SWEET
Agony

USA TODAY BESTSELLING AUTHOR
EMMANUELLE SNOW

Smart Lily
Publishing

Sweet Agony
Emmanuelle Snow

First edition - July 2021 (V_1)

ISBN eBook: 978-1-7776150-4-8

ISBN paperback: 978-1-990429-58-3

Previously published in 2021 as Princess and Country

Editors: Shalini G. and Stephanie Parent

Cover: SMART Lily publishing inc.

Published by SMART Lily Publishing inc.

———

Emmanuelle Snow
www.emmanuellesnow.com

CARTER HILLS BAND UNIVERSE
(SUGGESTED READING ORDER)

Carter Hills Band series
False Promises

HEART SONG DUET
BlindSided
ForeverMore

Whiskey Melody series
Sweet Agony

SECOND TEAR DUET
Cruel Destiny
Beautiful Salvation

BREATHLESS DUET
Wild Encounter
Brittle Scars

Upon A Star Series
Last Hope

Midnight Sparks

Love Song For Two Series
LONESOME STAR DUET
Fallen Legend
Rising Star

All titles available at
emmanuellesnow.com/books

For the best experience, read in the order as shown above

AUTHOR'S NOTE

This book has been previously published as ***Princess and Country***.

It's the same beautiful and emotionally-charged story about Dahlia Ellis growing up with the Hills brothers. It can be read as a standalone and it's part of the Whiskey Melody series.

For a better reading experience, read the ***Second Tear*** duet (***Cruel Destiny*** and ***Beautiful Salvation***) right after.

Happy reading!

Emmanuelle

WHAT THE REVIEWS SAY

- "If I could give more than 5 stars, I would."**(Jessica Belmont blog**)

- "Where has Emmanuelle Snow been hiding all my life?! It's the second book in the series and I'm still in love with her words." (**OMG Reads blog**)

- "Emmanuelle's magic lay in her words, and how she could squeeze my heart with a single stroke of her pen. It was magical. Not many authors could imbibe their words with emotions. This author could, and I was in awe." (**Book Reviews by Shalini**)

-" This is heartbreaking as much as it is heartwarming." (**Lili Blissful Pages**)

- "It was sweet, romantic, sad and all the feels. I laughed and cried." (**Goodreads review**)

- "This is a lovely romance that will tug at the heartstrings and keep you reading until the end." (**Red Pillows blog**)

- "There are twists and turns along with loss, betrayal, secrets, hope, love and so many emotional situations that I couldn't put this book down." (**Booksirens**)

- "Wow what a story so many emotions unraveling throughout where to begin." (**Booksirens**)

- "It has all the things you expect from a rockstar romance." (**Amazon customer**)

- "I would recommend reading it to those who enjoy a storyline with drama, emotional turmoil and challenges, and forever love." (**Booksirens**)

- "This is not a romance, it is a story about first love, first heartbreak and growing up. It is a story that helps to build foundation upon who someone is at their core, and what makes them strong, vulnerable, loving, caring and heart-broken but willing to take chances and learn to love again." (**JocelyneReadsRomance**)

TRIGGER WARNINGS

Disclaimer

My books are realistic and emotional romance reads.

I'm an advocate for mental health, and some topics could be sensitive for certain readers since they are portrayed as close to real life as possible.

I've listed the potential trigger warnings for each title on my website.

Be advised that those trigger warnings could potentially be spoiler alerts for the storylines.

Those sensitive topics have been written with the utmost care and respect. Please reach out if you have questions or comments.

All books contain sexuality, mature content, and language not intended for people under 18 years of age.
For other readers' sake, please avoid spoilers in your reviews.

Thank you and have a wonderful day!

Emmanuelle

emmanuellesnow.com/trigger-warnings

To my own little princesses.
You bring so much joy into my life.
Keep shining because your hearts are precious.

BECOME A VIP

TO NEVER MISS A THING

Snow's VIP

Join **Emmanuelle Snow's VIP newsletter** for all the cool stuff, promos, new releases, giveaways, and gifts.

emmanuellesnow.com/subscribe

Snow's Soulmates

Join Emmanuelle Snow's Facebook VIP group, **Snow's Soulmates**, to chat with her and other readers, get updates, and more bonus content.

facebook.com/groups/snowvip

HEART FOR RENT

THE SONG

I saw you first that day
Wearing a red dress
Your hair was flying around
    your face
Sunshine was brushing your skin
Lighting up your freckles like a road
    map to paradise
I stood there, frozen, mesmerized by
    your smile
I saw you first, girl

[CHORUS]
Your lips landed on mine
Your perfume washed over me
You promised me forever
You held my hand at night
But when the sun came out
You disappeared
Like the summer breeze, you just
    passed through my life

You weren't mine to keep
You weren't mine to hold
You weren't mine to love
I thought you gave me your heart
But realized it was only mine to rent

I ran after you
I called your number, at least a thou-
    sand times
I sat on your front porch every
    night, for months
But you never came back to me
Our love story wasn't meant to be
It was only good for a season

[CHORUS]

Fall bled into winter
The cold almost made me forget I'd
    ever had you
Spring came and went
I still see your face in my dreams
I still smell your perfume on my
    pillow
Did I make you up in my mind?
Please tell me it was real
Tell me it was real.

[CHORUS]

It's been years, but you're still on
    my mind
I thought I saw you the other day

With a ring around your finger, and
    him holding your hand
If only I had known your heart was
    only for rent
I might have held on to you stronger
    that night

Music and lyrics by Carter Hills

PROLOGUE
DAHLIA

Twenty years old

Hot tears etched their way down the delicate skin of my face. My heart leaped into my throat. I tried to scream. To expel all the fury broiling inside me. In vain. No sound came out of my mouth. Not even the sobs bubbling in the depths of me.

This day should've been one to remember. One to celebrate.

The happiest of my life so far. One to bring tears of joy to my eyes.

Instead…

I was a train wreck.

A ball of sadness.

A bomb about to explode.

Anger and grief twisted around, I didn't know where one ended and the other began.

How could this happen?

My day should've been blissful. Or I always thought

that was how it was supposed to be. I had no idea, as I'd never put too much thought into this before.

Right now, I had nothing to be festive about. I was about to shatter the heart of one of the two people I loved the most in this world. My insides roared into a blaze. Burning everything in their wake.

What had I done?

When my back landed on the wall behind me, I slid to the floor, curling into a ball.

I wrapped my arms around myself, trying to ease the pain. I wasn't sick. Not really. But the thought of breaking someone's heart—someone I loved most of all—was enough to draw me into a spiral of darkness.

I closed my eyes.

My breath caught in my lungs. I coughed, trying to get rid of the heaviness in my chest.

It wouldn't go away.

A soft knock on the door startled me.

"Hey, Dah, are you in here?" Jeff asked.

I said nothing. Because I had nothing to say, anyway.

He'd find out soon enough. I closed my trembling fist and let reality kick in.

I was down for the ride of my life.

I breathed. One. Two. Three. Time to face the music. Yeah, no pun intended.

Just life.

1

DAHLIA

Seven years old

Mama fixed my pigtails, and I put on my red dress, smoothing the silky fabric with my fingers. Today had to be perfect. Carter and I were doing our first real concert in the backyard. We practiced three songs—Johnny Cash, Garth Brooks, and Dolly Parton. The beating of my heart was weird, not calm and steady as usual.

"Mama, can my heart run away from my chest?"

"No, baby. Don't worry, you'll do great out there. Stress can be good. It happens to all your favorite country music idols too." Mama kneeled in front of me and pulled me in for a hug.

"Even Johnny?"

"Even Johnny, baby. It's okay to be scared. To be excited. Or both."

What was Mama even talking about? Since when was being afraid okay? Darkness, spiders, snakes. There was nothing fun about being scared of something.

Mama was wrong.

My heart raced in my chest, and a strong pinch hit my stomach every few minutes. With my eyes closed, I took a big whiff of Mama's perfume. Vanilla. I loved that smell. It always made everything better. Like the way I wrapped myself in one of Mama's sweaters when I was sick, sad, or tired.

Mama dropped a kiss on my forehead and got up.

At the doorway of my bedroom, she spun around and looked at me with her big blue-green eyes, bluer than mine, her red hair knotted at the back of her head. "You'll do great, baby. I believe in you."

My heart hiccupped in my chest.

"Carter's heart is in the right place. You two will be amazing together," Mama said. Why did she always tell me that? Wasn't everyone's heart in their chest? Or had I been wrong all along? I closed my eyes, hoping mine was in the right place too.

With both hands, I cupped it to make sure and breathed out. My heart was where it should be. My hands stayed glued to my chest, containing my heart inside, not willing to risk it moving around.

"Are you ready, Dah?" Carter asked as he walked into my bedroom. I spun a half-turn to greet him. His eyes widened at my sight. "Wow, you look pretty. Now I know why you insisted on wearing your red dress. It's like your hair is on fire." I twirled to show off my new dress, my copper pigtails flying at my sides. My best friend stuffed his hands in the pockets of his dark-blue denims, the ones he called his lucky pants. Carter Hills only wore jeans. Winter, summer, weekdays, weekends, that was all he ever wore. It suited him. In a way. Carter had been my best friend forever. Like we were the best of friends in the whole world.

I knew a secret about Carter, something I never revealed to him. Sometimes, he slept with his guitar in his bed. As if he considered it his friend too. I snickered just thinking about it. Carter didn't know I caught him the other morning with his arm wrapped around his guitar neck. I would never tell anybody. His secret was safe with me.

"Is your heart banging loud in your chest?" I asked him as I looked through my bedroom window. From here, I could see all eight people seated in garden chairs, facing the wooden stage Daddy built for us—the one I insisted he painted in purple, my favorite color. They were all there. My parents, Carter's parents, his older brother, Jeff, Addison—my other best friend—her twin brother Phoenix, and my nana.

"It did earlier. Not anymore. Because we're doing this together." Carter offered me his hand, and when our fingers laced together, a giant smile broke free on his face. "It's okay, Dah. I'm here. We can do this. Just follow my lead, I'll take care of everything."

My shoulders didn't feel so heavy now. I knew Carter was telling the truth. He would never let anything bad happen to me. Other than my parents and nana, Carter Hills was my *most favoritest* person in the entire world. I trusted him with everything.

When I was six, I was scared to swim in the big kids' pool at the sports center. Carter taught me how to hold my breath and swim with my head underwater.

And once, he carried me, piggyback, because I fell from the swing at the park and skinned my knee. Carter even dried my tears with the hem of his T-shirt that day and let me borrow Toby, his favorite stuffed monkey, for a week afterward.

Carter's eyes sparkled as he turned to face me. I

bobbed my head—just like the discolored frog that Daddy had on his car dash—and returned his smile.

"Let's go then." I grabbed my guitar from the little stand in the corner of my room. Last year, Daddy and I painted my bedroom walls purple, and they looked charming. Everything else was white. The comforter, the curtains, the small square rug, the dresser, and the fluffy chair by the window. Mama called it my Princess Kingdom.

One day, after school, when we were busy doing our homework, Carter said with a shrug, sitting cross-legged on my bed, "Dah, you should design beautiful things when you're grown up. You always make boring and ugly things pretty."

I liked the idea. Anything could be made beautiful with a little help. Even that chair my nana loved so much. We painted it pink and added a white satin cushion, and it turned out charming. *Charming* was my nana's way of saying amazing.

Carter grabbed the guitar from me, and with his left hand still glued to mine, we made it to the backyard. The warmth of his touch helped to keep my heart from doing gymnastics in my chest.

Daddy, with a huge grin splitting his face, set two folding chairs on the stage and placed a single microphone on a stand in front of us. Mama had hung garden lights above the stage, and Jeff helped with the setup. Carter's brother was ten, so he was a lot stronger than Carter and me. He always volunteered to help us out. Jeff was Carter's other best friend.

Nobody talked when we sat. Was I supposed to hear my own breathing? I closed my eyes and ran my hands over my red dress. Birds chirped in the trees, and the sound of a lawnmower across the street broke the silence. I opened my eyes when I felt gazes on me. Everyone was staring at us. My mouth went dry. My eyes burned. My throat closed. Carter placed his hand on my thigh, and as if he spread magic through me, I relaxed.

"Don't look at them, Dah. Look at me. I'm right here."

A wide smile brightened his face. Carter loved to perform. The sound of his voice gave me goosebumps. My eyes rested on his. The gray irises—the same color as the sky before a storm—tousled dark hair—he never took the time to comb—his beautiful face—that always calmed me down. Carter was my safe place in choppy times. Even when he always looked as if he just woke up with the wind in his hair, which I thought was funny. Now my fingers itched to brush the strands away from his forehead.

I pinched my lips together, drew a deep breath, and without a word, I nodded. I could do this. We'd rehearsed those three songs at least twenty times. Jeff heard us play one night and told us we were pretty great. He was older and knew more about life than us. If he said so, then maybe we were.

My eyes drifted to the small crowd.

Jeff locked his eyes on mine and gave me a small smile and a thumbs-up.

I inhaled through my nose, like my nana taught me to do when my heart beat too fast, and rolled my shoulders back.

Carter struck the first chord, and my throat relaxed. *Yes, I can do this.* A mantra I told myself as the first words left my mouth.

My eyes stayed on Carter the entire time my fingers strummed my guitar. He had a permanent smile on his lips as he sang with me all through the three songs.

Jeff was right. We were pretty great.

———

Ten years old

"One day, we'll be at the top of the world," Carter announced with a huge smile as he stepped on an old empty wooden crate at the back of his garage, holding his guitar above his head like some sort of trophy. His garage was our rehearsing space. His daddy cleaned out a corner for us to rehearse after school, on weekends, and during the summer. With Jeff's help—because he knew how to use the big stapler and the stepladder—I hung fairy lights across the ceiling. We used old furniture some neighbors were getting rid of to furnish our corner. Carter hung a Johnny Cash frame on one wall, and I brought my glittery pink blanket to cover the ugly-brown-stained sofa Mrs. Canterbury, our seventy-six-old neighbor, had gifted us. Mrs. Canterbury loved our music and often asked Carter and me to play for her in exchange for cookies and home-made lemonade. Who could ever refuse such a deal? Not us. We loved cookies way too much. So, mostly on hot summer days, we played for our neighbor—which meant an endless supply of snacks and lemonade. Sweet deal because Tennessee summers were hot as hell, as Mama often said.

"We'll have people cheering for us," I said. "Imagine if we could have twenty people coming over to listen to us. It would be huge. We could make flyers and ask the postman to pass them to the neighborhood. Or maybe we could give them out at the grocery store ourselves."

Carter shook his head. "No, Dah, we'll fill a stadium. Like the one where we went to see the monster trucks competition the other day with your daddy."

"A stadium?" My heart made a funny flip in my chest. "I don't know, Carter. Won't you be nervous if strangers come to see you sing? A stadium means a lot of people.

Like a lot. At least a thousand. I'm not sure I want that. It'll be scary. Twenty people are already one too many. Don't you think it's a big enough crowd?"

"My daddy always says to dream big. I think twenty people is not enough, Dah." Carter shook his head, still perched on that wooden crate. "We need to aim bigger. How about a hundred people? It would be huge if we could play for that many people."

My breath got stuck in my lungs, and I coughed. I rubbed my hands together. Carter's head needed to be checked. Could he be suffering from a heat stroke? I should go inside and get his mama. One hundred people? Carter looked at me with big, rounded eyes. Was he serious? "A hundred people? Carter, I'm not even sure Johnny Cash had that many people coming to see him in a concert. If we can get fifty people to pay for tickets to hear us, we'll be rich and famous."

Carter pondered my words for a couple of beats. "You're right. If we get fifty people to buy ten-buck tickets, we'll be superstars."

I emptied my lungs. Okay, fifty was better than one hundred. I could do fifty. Or I hoped I could. The flip-flops in my chest returned.

———

Fourteen years old

"Hey, Dah. Guess what?" I turned to come face-to-face with an overenthusiastic Carter. His stormy-gray eyes lit up the school hallway. My best friend had gotten taller over the summer and was now towering over me by at least six inches. I had to tilt my head back to look him in the eyes if we stood too close to each other.

Today he wore his faded, ripped-at-the-knees black jeans and a fitted black T-shirt underneath a plaid red shirt. His usual outfit. Carter raked his hands through his mass of untamed dark brown hair. I inched closer to him and lifted my hand to comb the wild strands with my fingers. He bent his head forward to help me reach the back of his head. A shiver ran from him through me as I massaged his scalp. It vibrated from my fingertips to my belly.

"Here you go," I said, my voice lower than I wanted it to be. Carter cleared his throat and averted his gaze. Lately, whenever we were alone, Carter looked at me in a way he never had before. I didn't know what to think of it. We told each other everything, but this… this was huge. I was afraid to know what it meant. His eyes darkened, and his lips formed a thin line. It sent some strange fuzzy feeling down to my belly.

Phoenix and Addison, our joined-at-the-hips twin friends, passed us in the hallway. Phoenix clapped Carter's shoulder. "Still on for tonight?" he asked, waiting for Carter's reply. Phoenix was a wide receiver for the football team and organized parties all the time. Most times, I wasn't allowed to attend. But here and there, if Carter was with me, Mama agreed to let me go.

"It depends on if Dah can come," Carter said with his usual I-don't-care shrug.

His eyes traveled to me, telling me we didn't have to go if I preferred doing something else.

I blinked and hoped Carter got it. We were good at understanding each other without words. Through our silent exchange, I didn't miss the look in Addison's eyes. She'd had a thing for my best friend for about a year now. Addi thought Carter was mysterious and hot. To me, he was none of those things. For me, Carter was smart, focused, and caring. Every time he was around, my girl-friend became mute, her cheeks flushed, and she kept her head down, not meeting his eyes. Carter was clueless about her crush. And since he and I were also joined at the hips, Addison thought I was always in the way. But Carter was my best friend, and I was his. Nothing could change that. I didn't want Addi asking him out because I preferred having him all to myself, so I told her I refused to play a part in setting them up. The idea of my two best friends dating and kissing made me gag.

No, thanks.

"Mama said I could go, only if you're there and we come home before ten. But I promised my nana I'd visit her after school, so I might be late."

"I'll come see her with you," Carter said, staring at me, his hands shoved in his pockets. A wave of heat ran down my spine.

Carter twisted his upper body to face the twins. "It's settled. We'll meet you guys later."

Phoenix nodded and tugged at his sister's hand. "C'mon, Addi, we'll be late."

"See you later, Dah." Addison waggled her fingers at me.

"So, where were we? Oh yes. My big news." Carter clutched my shoulders. "Mark's father owns a radio station in Nashville. Mark told him about the music festival we did last summer and the offer we got to play at the town Halloween bash. Anyway, his dad wants to interview us. Sometime next month."

"You're kidding, right?" Carter's grin widened—as if that could even be possible—and he shook his head. "Wow, I don't know what to say." A truckload of thoughts bounced around in my head. "You sure we're ready for that kind of publicity?" A tightness grew around my heart, and my hands became moist. Could I handle all the attention?

"This is our chance. We should practice this song we've been working on in case he asks us to play something. It's better if we come up with something original, don't you think?"

I nodded. My thoughts raced around. It took me a minute to process the news.

"That's—I lack words. Can you gimme some time to deal with it? A radio interview is kinda big. And I'm not a sucker for being in the spotlight."

Carter intertwined our fingers. "It'll be okay, Dah. I'll be right by your side. Just follow my lead, and I'll take care of everything."

How could I not trust my best friend? For years, he'd repeated those same exact words to me anytime I was nervous performing.

And never once had Carter failed to fulfill his promise to protect and care for me.

As long as I had him in my corner, I was safe.

Around midnight, dressed in dark green sleep shorts and an oversized black T-shirt that belonged to Carter, I waited, cross-legged on my bed, in the dark. I knew he was coming. Like he'd been doing every few nights for the last seven years.

Flutters danced in my tummy when I heard the knock on the window. Carter's head peeked between the white curtains.

"What took you so long?" I asked as I slid under the covers and flipped down the left side for him to join me.

"Dad and Jeff were still up, arguing about a party Jeff went to. Something about booze. Anyway, I had to wait until they were both in their rooms to escape."

Thanks to the high silvery moon outside, I noticed twinkles in my best friend's eyes.

"Why are you so happy?"

Carter shrugged. "No reason. I'm always happier when I'm with you."

In plaid blue pajama pants and a white T-shirt, he joined me in my bed. We'd been having secret sleepovers for so long it wasn't even awkward to share a bed. Carter lay on his back and grabbed my hand in his, holding tight. I shifted on the mattress until our heads pressed against each other.

"Good night, Cart."

"Night, Dah."

With my best friend by my side, I fell asleep knowing nothing could ever harm me.

2

DAHLIA

Fifteen years old

"I'm almost done with this math homework. Are you still on for rehearsal tonight?" I asked Carter as he lay on my bedspread, on his stomach, his legs crossed at the ankles. He looked good as he focused on the paper in front of him. His hair, now longer, reached mid-ears, which I liked a lot.

Last year, after our radio interview with Mark's father, which got us a dozen gigs in the following months, Carter decided we should write our own songs. We were good at coming up with melodies, but putting words around those chords turned out to be a tedious task. I wasn't that interested in this side of music, but Carter had the will and talent to write lyrics. He loved poetry and had always got straight As in composition for English class. In the last four months, Carter had come up with two original songs. We now had three including the one he wrote last year that we played at the radio interview.

My eyes took him in as he chewed on his ballpoint pen, oblivious to anything I said.

As I leaned closer, Carter snapped out of his daze and met my eyes. His turned darker as they gave me a once-over. A sly smile appeared at the corner of his lips. My eyes lingered on his mouth. A few months back, I'd started wondering if Carter would ever kiss me. Some days I wanted him to. And some days, I thought it would be weird. I'd never kissed anyone before, but would kissing my best friend feel like kissing my own brother? Not that I had a brother, though. But Carter was the closest thing to a sibling that I had. Ugh. I had mixed feelings about my attraction to him. Every time his eyes locked on mine though, my heart raced in my chest.

I loved and feared the sensation.

All the girls at school now noticed him too. But Carter turned them down when they asked him on dates or fought to get his attention.

And I'd noticed something else.

Carter never looked at any of those girls the same way he looked at me. With some sort of fondness in his eyes. And I had no idea why.

We had this strong chemistry going on between us. Could I be wrong about Carter's feelings toward me? Our friendship was so powerful; it overpowered my rational thoughts.

The other night, we went to the movies with a bunch of our friends, and Carter held my hand the entire night as if he were afraid I'd vanish. My heart drummed in my chest for hours afterward. I thought he'd say something to me on our way back—or the next day—but nothing. My best friend was giving me mixed signals.

Carter, still lying on my bed, gave me a quizzical stare.

"Sorry, got lost for a moment," I said. A warm flush crept up my cheeks.

He tipped my chin up with his finger. "Everything all right, Dah?"

I bobbed my head. Like a stupid girl with a forbidden crush. "Sure. Was wondering if you were still on for rehearsal tonight."

"Yeah. I'm stuck. I can't write this song, anyway." Carter smiled at me, and my pulse accelerated. I breathed faster.

Carter Hills was sweet, generous, and ambitious. Would kissing him put our relationship at risk? Or would I one day feel his lips on mine, his hands around my waist, and his heart beating against mine?

I chased the thought away, feeling ridiculous.

"I'm done with my homework. I'll meet you at your place in an hour."

Carter brushed a strand of my copper hair away from my forehead. Tingles lined my spine.

"Sure," he said, jumping to his feet. He adjusted his shirt and ran downstairs. From the living-room window, I watched him as he walked away, my insides coiled in a tight knot and a prickling sensation at the back of my neck. Warmth rushed to my cheeks. Growing up was so confusing.

———

Six months later

Tonight, I was having dinner at the Hills'. Like most Tuesdays and Wednesdays. I was sitting alone at the kitchen counter working on a project, Carter busy helping his daddy in the garage and his mama on the phone in her home office. Jeff came home fifteen minutes ago and went straight upstairs. He didn't even say hi as he walked past me. I watched his back as he padded away and furrowed my eyebrows. This was rude. We weren't friends like Carter and me, but I still considered him family.

Kind of.

With glue, Styrofoam balls, paint, and wooden sticks, I was putting the last few touches on Carter and my science project, a three-dimensional DNA model. Carter assembled the entire thing last night to surprise me. And it looked better than I ever thought it would.

He must have worked on this for hours. Did he even sleep?

Jeff came downstairs in a white towel hanging low around his hips, and his dark hair—the same shade as Carter's but shorter—wet, pearls of water dripping over his bare chest. The moment he appeared, my eyes bulged, and I almost fell off my stool. I did my best not to ogle at him and sipped my water to hide what I was sure were bright-red, flaming cheeks. But how could I keep my gaze from traveling to his muscled chest? I noticed the small tattoo over his left pec—some sort of symbol—and wondered what it meant. When did he get inked? I knew nothing about this grown-up version of Jeff Hills. Was the tattoo there last summer when we all spent a weekend at the beach? No. I would have noticed it. Wouldn't I? Even if I hated tattoos, on Jeff, the inking looked fierce. And hot.

Forbidden.

And badass.

Jeff sauntered across the kitchen, and I admired every inch of him. Not as tall as Carter, but close enough, he had broader shoulders, and his skin was golden, like he'd spent the day under the sun. He worked out a lot, and it showed. He grabbed a bottle of water from the refrigerator, and my eyes drifted to the damp footprints he left in his wake. Jeff pivoted on his heels, and I held my breath when he looked my way. His gaze burned my skin. I failed at reading his expression. His eyes, darker than usual, turned almost black. For a long second, he scanned the length of me, chugging the entire bottle in one gulp. I swallowed hard, staring at the working column of his throat, my eyes following a drop of water as it made its way down his neck.

As he padded out of the kitchen, Jeff winked my way, his face still unreadable, and I thought I'd melt on the tiled white floor. I fanned myself with my hand, trying to find my composure. My insides turned into a scorching puddle of molten wax.

What just happened?

I dragged a shaky hand over my face, unsure of what I'd just witnessed.

Carter joined me as his brother disappeared upstairs, brushing my upper arm with his long fingers. "You okay? You're flushed. Are you having a fever?" His hand found my forehead. "No. You're fine. What's wrong?"

My pulse picked up. I hated lying to him. We were always honest with each other. Carter told me all about that time Addison cornered him in the locker room after gym class and kissed him. I confided in him when I got my period and when I needed to buy a bra for the first time. But this? I couldn't find it in me to tell him about my heated encounter with Jeff. Never would I allow myself to go crazy over my best friend's older brother. This was just wrong. And it would crush Carter's heart. And his heart was precious and rare. Like a priceless diamond.

At fifteen, I now knew what Mama meant this entire time when she said Carter's heart was in the right place.

"It's hot in here," I said. Lame. Pathetic. In my head, I slapped myself as the words came out.

Carter shrugged. "I'll adjust the air-conditioning. Next time, don't be silly, ask Mama or Jeff if I'm not around. Or do it yourself. It's super easy." Carter rose to his feet and toyed with the temperature control. "There. All set." He took his place at the kitchen counter beside me. "Sorry, I'm late. Let's finish this project before dinner." I nodded, agreeing with the more-than-welcome change of subject.

During dinner, I deliberately sat beside Jeff, at the table, opposite Carter. I wouldn't be distracted or get caught staring at his brother if we sat on the same side of the table.

"Can you pass me the salt?" Jeff asked me once we all dug into our food.

Our fingers brushed, and some electric current traveled through me. I sucked in a breath and heard Jeff do the same. The saltshaker fell from my grip, and in a quick movement, I dropped my hand in my lap, hoping to hide my trembling fingers.

What's happening to me?

My heart banged in my chest, and I feared it would land on the table for everyone to see.

Carter kicked my shin from under the table.

"Are you okay?" he mouthed.

I mouthed a "yes," keeping my gaze low. Why was Carter always so perceptive to everything concerning me? He knew me like nobody else did. He could read me even when I was struggling to come to terms with my own emotions.

I forced a small smile his way, and he returned it.

My eyes said, *I'm okay*, and I crossed my fingers behind my back, hoping he couldn't figure it out.

His said, *You can tell me if something's bothering you*, along with a fleeting expression I had a hard time figuring out. Could he tell I was smitten with his brother? I had no idea.

Jeff pressed his thigh against mine under the table, and I was pretty sure my heart stopped. I died right there. Was he messing with me on purpose? Did he feel the electricity between us when we touched?

"Hey, Mama, dinner is amazing tonight," Jeff said. "I'm glad I didn't skip it like I was supposed to. I think I should eat here, with all of you, more often." His thigh pressed harder against mine. Was that a cocky grin on his lips? I drowned my uneasiness with a sip of water but ended up choking. Tears welled in my eyes as I coughed, my lungs burning. Jeff turned his upper body toward me and rubbed my back. With gentleness. His warmth shot through me. When my cough subsided, I cocked my head his way.

"Thanks," I said in such a low, croaky voice, I feared he wouldn't hear me. His hand lingered on my back another minute, and we glanced at each other longer than we should have, neither of us breaking our eye contact. I pressed my lips together as big knots tied my stomach.

"I couldn't let you drown over a gulp of water, Princess," Jeff said, using the nickname he gave me when we were kids and I refused to jump into a mud hole, wearing my favorite white dress and glittery silver shoes.

I forced a small curl on my lips and brought my attention back to my dinner. Carter missed the entire exchange between his brother and me, deep in a conversation about some hockey stats with his daddy.

Mrs. Hills cleared her throat, and when I looked her way, she beamed, offering me a warm smile I'd never got before. I'd always suspected Jeff was her favorite child. Not that any parent should have one, though. But Mrs. Hills was much more enthusiastic about Jeff's antics than she was about Carter's musical talent. Jeff held a special place in her heart. One I'd never fully understand. He could get away with pretty much anything.

Mrs. Hills cleared her throat. "Dahlia, dear, could you help Jeff clean the table? It's his turn, and I need to discuss something with Carter." I bobbed my head in agreement as I rose from my seat.

"Mama, we can talk later. Don't make Dahlia do my chore." There. Carter. Always thinking about me. Putting my needs first. Making me his priority. Protecting me.

"It's okay, Cart. I can do this. I'm eating here all the time. And you always do the dishes with my daddy when you come over. Let me do this."

Carter grabbed my hand as I picked up his plate. "You sure?" he asked, so low only I could hear him. I nodded. We exchanged a small smile, and I followed Jeff into the kitchen. Once again, my heart went wild in my chest. My body temperature rose, and despite the air-conditioning, molten lava coursed through my veins. I stood beside Jeff, and neither of us said anything as he washed and I dried. A few times, our arms brushed each other, and the same zipping sensation I felt during dinner ran through me. I held my breath as long as I could, hoping it would settle my heart down. It didn't work. I stepped to my left, leaving a gap between Jeff's body and mine, needing to reset my boundaries. And calm my nerves. Seconds later, Jeff stepped to the left too, erasing the distance between us. As if he needed to be close to me. Or as if my body attracted his.

All my thoughts jumbled inside my head.

With my mouth clamped shut, I kept my eyes glued to the dishcloth in my hands and zoomed in on my task of drying up plates, glasses, bowls, pots, and pans.

When I fumbled to place the salad bowl away on the

highest shelf, Jeff held my hips from behind with a feather touch, moving me to the side. My knees weakened.

"Let me do this," he offered, his voice hoarse, his breath tickling my nape. Shivers ran through me. "Are you cold?" I shook my head, avoiding his eyes.

"No. I'm fine." I forced the words out.

We breathed the same air for a full minute, neither of us breaking the awkward silence, before we finished putting all the dishes away.

Once we were done, Jeff gave me one last heated glance and disappeared upstairs.

He never came back down as Carter and I moved to the garage to rehearse the song we'd been working on for the last week.

―――――

"I had another moment with Jeff the other night," I told Addison as we were getting our nails done. A treat her mother gifted us since she owned the place. "You should have seen him when he was fixing his truck. All sweaty. Never before have I felt like this looking at a guy's glistening chest. I'm telling you, there were butterflies flying around in my stomach."

"Again? OMG, Dah, are you serious? Do you know if he's attracted to you?"

I sighed. A warmth spread all over my face. "I don't know. Why would a senior be interested in a freshman? I bet he thinks I'm just a kid, and he enjoys messing with me. I'm sure he knows he's hot. Girls are throwing themselves at his feet, hoping he'll ask one of them to be his prom date. I can't compete."

"What does Carter think about you crushing on his big brother?" I buried my face in my free hand at the question, and a loud groan escaped my lips. "You didn't tell him?" Her words expounded my guilt.

I lowered my shoulders. "No. I think Carter might love me. Emotions and everything. There's something different in the way he's been looking at me. Like nobody else but me exists in his world. Like I'm his world. If he does love me—like *love*, love me—it complicates things."

"What do you mean?"

"Sure, I love Carter. Like a lot. More than I should. But Jeff makes my insides vibrate. I can't breathe when he's around. And I can't look at him, worried he'd see through me. But I'm sure he only sees me as his brother's friend. Anyway, he'll be in college soon. I'm being ridiculous."

Addison pushed her baby-blonde hair over her shoulder and batted her dark eyelashes, making kissing sounds. I poked my tongue out at her and wrinkled my nose.

"You're so screwed, girlfriend."

She burst out laughing, and after a few seconds, I joined in. Addi was right. My crush on Jeff would get me into trouble.

My laughter died and I sighed.

My heart sank in my chest. I was pining over my best friend's older brother like a groupie. And I was pretty sure my best friend was pining over me. I could already sense the disaster and pain coming my way.

"If Carter had a thing for me, we could have gone on a double date," my girlfriend said in a dreamy voice. "But you two are possessive about each other. Always have been. No wonder you never helped me out when I was obsessed with him."

I grimaced. "Sorry—"

"Don't worry. I kissed him, and he freaked out. We

weren't meant to be, and I'm happy with Chris. He's funny. And at least, Phoenix doesn't want to kill him since he's his friend. Not like with Darren. Now back to you. What are you gonna do?"

"I don't know." I truly had no idea what to do with my messy feelings for my best friend's older brother.

Addi burst out laughing. "I can't wait to see how you'll get out of this one, Dah."

I nudged her upper arm, and her laughter picked up.

Thanks for the support, girlfriend.

3

DAHLIA

"Thanks for driving us, bro," Carter told Jeff when we were on our way to play at Country Fest, a music festival thirty miles south of our hometown and twenty minutes east of Nashville.

Jeff shrugged from the driver's seat. "Anytime, guys. You're talented. I'm happy to help you out whenever I can. Anyway, Brendan and a few guys will join me later to watch you play." In the backseat, I stayed quiet. Quieter than usual. I kept a low profile, admiring the scenery through the window.

It'd been three weeks since that dinner where I realized I had it bad for Jeff. When my body ignited for the first time in his presence.

From that day on, I tried my best to avoid him as much as possible. Carter told me his brother had never been home so often as in the last month. Each time Mrs. Hills invited me to stay over, I found a million reasons to go back home. Yeah, I'd become this pathetic version of myself.

And each time, Carter begged me to stay with those stormy eyes of his. The ones I had a hard time resisting.

Addison and I had also been spending more time together in the last few weeks. She volunteered to be my distraction as often as possible. To keep me away from the Hills' household. For my heart's safety, as she claimed.

We both knew it was bullshit, but I was grateful for her efforts. Maybe if I stayed away from Jeff, my growing feelings for him would go away on their own. Maybe I'd grow some sort of armor, and his presence wouldn't affect me anymore.

There was no harm in a little wishful thinking.

When Carter told me Jeff would be driving us today instead of his daddy, I wanted to fake a sickness. Or a voice loss. Anything to keep me at a safe distance from his brother.

Carter pivoted his upper body from the passenger seat and studied me. "Are you anxious, Dah? You're not saying anything. Usually, when you're nervous before a show, you can't stop rambling."

I plastered a smile on my face, doing my best to hide how I felt inside—my best friend was too good at reading me. "Yeah. I'm perfect. Just tired, that's all. Don't worry."

I averted my gaze but ended up being sucked into Jeff's dark irises as he stared at me through the rearview mirror. I tried hard, but I couldn't swallow. Did my throat shrink in the last hour? I slid my shaky hands under my thighs, hiding my fidgeting from my best friend and his brother.

Jeff's heated stare melted me in my seat. A pool of warmth rose into my cheeks. My spine tingled. I parted my lips to say something, but every word froze on the tip of my tongue.

Jeff's eyes captured mine the entire ride. Whatever I did to avoid him, it didn't work because my gaze met his every single time. Jeff had gained control of my body.

Whatever he did, I hovered in his direction. He was a magnet, and I was made of steel.

Weak and malleable steel.

I flipped my copper hair over my shoulder. It curled into soft waves down my back. Jeff muttered something I didn't catch from the backseat.

My breath stuck in my lungs.

"Did you say something?" Carter asked, raising his eyes from his phone screen, bringing his attention to his brother.

"No. Just cleared my throat." Jeff and I exchanged a look through the mirror. He was lying.

My skin itched.

My insides dissolved.

My heart thundered.

For once, I wasn't anxious about the show we were about to give, my mind too busy avoiding Jeff Hills.

"Okay, guys, we're here," he told us as he parked his gray pickup truck near the musicians' entrance. Carter gave us each a pass to put around our neck.

His brother helped us unload our guitars and stuff from the cargo bed.

"Hey, Dahlia—" My heartbeat went up. Fast. No "Princess" this time. Jeff reached for my hand, and his fingers skimmed mine. "—watch over my brother, would you?"

I nodded, my mouth as dry as sandpaper and my heart flipping in my chest. "Sure. Always."

Jeff offered me a tight-lipped smile, and I forced myself to orbit out of his magnetic field.

"We'll be playing at six-thirty," Carter informed him, oblivious to every word exchanged between his brother and me. "It's not even noon, so we'll have time to rehearse

some more. Do you want to meet us before our set to grab
a bite?"

"Sure. But I think I'll hang with you guys in the mean-
time. I love watching you play. I've been doing it since you
were seven-year-old kids. I consider myself your oldest and
biggest fan."

Jeff's grin woke up something in me I couldn't ignore.
Spending our day with him didn't seem like such a good
idea. Would I even be able to focus on my music if he was
around?

Carter draped an arm around his brother's shoulders,
pulling him into a hug.

"Yes, you are. I love you, big brother."

"Love you too, little bro."

Carter and Jeff were as close as Carter and I were.

If I had any doubt my crush—which I feared was now
reciprocated—for Jeff was messy, it had just got messier.
Someone—one of us—would suffer from a broken heart
soon. And I wasn't ready for it to happen.

We retreated backstage around six, and Jeff left to meet
with his friends.

"I'll see you guys later. Go, do your thing. I'll cheer you
from the crowd."

Jeff would be watching us—watching me. Why didn't it
occur to me earlier? My heart leaped into my throat. I
couldn't breathe. With my eyes closed, I inhaled through
my mouth to loosen the knots around my stomach.

———

A week later

After I searched the first floor, I ran upstairs, looking for
my best friend. I had some great news that I couldn't wait

to share. Mr. Hills, whom I ran into in the driveway, told me Carter was in the house, somewhere. Once my feet landed on the second floor, I hurried to his bedroom. I peeked inside. No trace of Carter either.

Noises came from the bathroom.

The door was open, so I rushed inside. I hit a wall. A human wall, made of skin and muscles. And I almost fell back on my ass. I lifted my eyes and came face-to-face with Jeff. The warmth of his hand spread through my core. I hadn't even noticed he gripped my waist, preventing me from falling after I bumped into him.

"Hey you," he said as a greeting. My words jammed in my throat. "Are you okay? Did you bump your head?" I was speechless, my feet glued to the floor. "Dahlia?"

I found my voice. "I'm okay. My head is fine." That's when I realized Jeff was only wearing black boxer briefs. I tried to keep my eyes level with his, but I failed. They traveled down his body on their own, taking their own sweet time. I took in the corded forearms, the ripped chest, his tight abs, the muscular thighs. The bulge in his boxers twitched, and I looked away. When my eyes landed back on his, a sly smirk lit up his face.

"Were you looking for me? Or are you trying to catch a sight of me?" Jeff arched one dark brow, and I had to hold on to him to avoid falling. Collapsing. Liquifying. Dying.

"Carter—I'm looking for Carter." My voice sounded too high-pitched and weird.

"He went to the store with Mom. He should be back soon. You want to hang out here?"

I should've said no.

I should've left.

But I stayed.

"Sure. But only if you get dressed first." I grimaced.

Then shut my eyes because I knew I was making a fool of myself. Did I catch fire? Was my face combusting?

A loud, deep chuckle escaped Jeff's throat. The sound of it calmed the storm raging inside me. It soothed me. I inhaled through my mouth.

"Great. Follow me."

Jeff tugged my hand and led the way to his bedroom. My hand tingled in his. My teeth nibbled my bottom lip.

My heels dug in the floor, inches away from the threshold.

Would I be able to keep breathing?

Jeff turned around. "Don't worry, I won't scare you away. I've got this playlist I made, and I'm sure you'll like it. Just sit on my bed, I'll be right back."

I nodded. Because I was at a loss for words. I must have looked like a complete idiot. When I realized my jaw hung open, I clamped it shut.

"Wait here." Jeff left his room, leaving me alone. I'd never been in here before. Carter's room was decorated with music band posters and his guitars.

Jeff's room was different, though. It had bare charcoal walls with white trim, dumbbells stacked beside his bed, a computer on his wall-length desk, and a navy-blue comforter. It was masculine. Raw. And smelled like Jeff. Sandalwood. And cinnamon.

I sat on the edge of the bed, fidgeting with a corner of the comforter. Just being here, in Jeff's room, felt like I was cheating on Carter. Like I'd entered enemy territory. My heart skipped many beats when Jeff returned in a white V-neck T-shirt, stretching across his defined chest—and clinging to his biceps—and light blue jeans, hugging his thighs and rear lovingly, and took a seat beside me, offering me a can of Coke and placing a bowl of tortilla chips on the desk.

"Thanks," I said.

Jeff's long jean-covered leg brushed mine.

Static flared between us.

Tightness grew around my heart. The butterflies in my stomach multiplied.

We stayed side by side for a long minute, neither of us breaking the silence, sipping our drinks.

Once my nerves settled—sort of—I breathed in some air and courage. "About that playlist—"

Jeff's eyes lit up. "Yeah. Sure. Don't move." He sat at his desk and switched on the computer. I missed the warmth of his thigh against mine the second he rose to his feet. He clicked on a few tabs, and the music, a song I didn't recognize, started playing from the speakers on each side of the screen.

Bonding over music erased some of the tension in the room.

As time passed, we made ourselves more comfortable.

Little knots in my stomach loosened.

We shared smiles. And Jeff was right; I adored his playlist.

"I didn't you know you like indie music—"

"There is a lot of things you don't know about me, Princess," he said, his eyes zeroing on mine, all traces of playfulness now gone.

That was it. The moment I'd die. Did my lungs puncture, or was I having a heart attack? Anyhow, something didn't feel right in my chest. I closed my eyes and swallowed hard, my breathing slowly evening out.

When I opened my eyes, Jeff's gaze was still trained on me.

"You want to make one?" he asked.

My lips parted, but I said nothing.

I must have looked at him with question marks in my

eyes because he added, "A playlist? You want to make one?"

"I'm—I'm not sure how," I said in a low voice, avoiding the magnetism of his irises.

"It's super easy. I'll show you. Here, take my seat."

Jeff tugged at my hand, and I got up to sit on the chair he had just vacated. He kneeled beside me and handled the mousepad, blanketing my hand with his large one, his skin feeling soft on mine. Jeff's scent enveloped me. I closed my eyes and took a big whiff. Better.

Each time our skin brushed, my heart swelled a bit more in my chest.

Time passed, and after a while, I forgot about my big news.

Wherever Carter was, he still wasn't home.

On his bed, Jeff rested his back against the wall, his legs stretched in front of him as I lay on my front, my chin propped on my crossed arms, beside him.

The silence felt comfortable. My heart had decreased its thunderous beating.

"I can't believe we've never had a chance to hang out together," Jeff said after a while. "You and Carter are always together. Like Siamese twins. He's so protective of you."

I swiveled my head to stare at him. His posture was more relaxed than before.

"Carter's my best friend. I've never pictured you as the guy hanging out with his younger brother's friends. Carter's your—"

Jeff straightened his back and peeled himself from the wall. "I don't care about your age, Dahlia. We've been around each other forever. I've never considered you to be only my brother's friend."

The air around us changed in a second. Seriousness

flashed in his eyes. Jeff gazed at me with an intensity that seared my being. I lost myself in the hypnotic pull of his irises. Neither of us blinked. Neither looked away. The pounding of my heart made me dizzy.

"Here you are," Carter announced as he walked into the room, breaking the moment. "Dad told me you were here. I'm sorry it took longer than expected. There was a fender-bender on the highway." My best friend sat on the bed next to me, unaware of the connection simmering between his brother and me, and continued, "What are you guys doing?" I rose to sit on my heels, hoping to find my balance after the avalanche of overwhelming emotions.

"Listening to music," Jeff shrugged, "waiting for you to come home. You're lucky I was around when your sorry ass wasn't," he ended with a wink. Carter captured Jeff in a headlock, and they brawled, laughing like idiots, until they rolled off the bed and crashed on the floor, never breaking apart.

The memory of why I came here returned.

"Hey, Cart, when you're done, I have something to tell you. It's big." Carter released his grip on his brother, my words acting like a fight breaker. His eyes flared as he rested on all fours, on the hardwood floor. He tipped his eyebrows, prompting me to speak up. From the corner of my eye, I noticed Jeff looking my way with the same curiosity, both Hills brothers ready to swallow anything I had to say.

Feeling self-conscious, I adjusted my shirt and pushed my thick braid over my shoulder.

My eyes met Jeff's for a flash before stopping on Carter. I couldn't seem to look directly into his eyes. My gaze slipped down a little, a sliver of guilt prickling inside me. Both stared at me like I held the truth to eternal life.

I cleared my throat, chasing my doubts away. "You

know Maurice, the European guy working with Daddy?"
Carter nodded. My eyes landed on Jeff again. He stole all
the air from my lungs. I shut my eyes for a second—or two
—trying to regain my composure. "Well, he opened a
restaurant on Main Street and asked if we'd consider
playing there every Saturday night. There's a stage in the
back." Carter looked at me with wide eyes and a slack-
ening jaw. "What do you think? The pay isn't bad either. If
it works out, he might open a second restaurant within a
year in Nashville, and he'd sometimes send us there to
play." Carter stayed silent. All the hair rose on my arms. I
thought this was huge. Why wasn't Carter saying anything?
"Cart?"

He snapped out of his daze and rushed toward me,
lifting me from the floor. My best friend spun me around.
"Did I ever tell you how much I love you?" A thick silence
fell over the room. After Carter put me back on my feet,
my eyes searched Jeff's. He stood there, back firmed, chin
high, his left hand rubbing the nape of his neck.

How I wished, right now, it was him spinning me
around, his lips uttering those words?

My feelings were a jumbled mess.

I swallowed the boulder-sized lump forming in my
throat, pushing the chaos building inside me as deep as I
could.

Jeff unfroze and neared his brother. They fist-bumped.
"Hey, that's great news, man. I guess that's going to be our
new hangout spot on Saturday nights from now on. I hope
it's not a five-star joint." Jeff winked, and we all erupted
into a fit of giggles. Some of the tension in the room
evaporated.

"We need to meet him on Wednesday night. My daddy
will drive us." Carter's smile reached his ears.

Sparks erupted inside my chest.

"We should get ready. Let's rehearse our new song again tonight. There're some adjustments I want to make," he said.

Carter pushed me forward, his hand between my shoulder blades.

I stopped in the doorway and turned around. Jeff stood there, his eyes following us—following me—as if he had no idea what to do next.

"Thanks for spending time with me," I said. "And thanks for helping me with the playlist. I'll send it to you when it's done, so you can tell me what you think of it."

He shoved his hands in his pockets and bowed his head.

My heart vibrated in my chest.

My eyes lingered on his throat, trying to catch sight of his pulse, wondering if it matched mine?

I waved at Jeff, and his lips curled up in the most amazing smile. One I'd never seen him give anybody else. Not even his ex-girlfriend.

Shivers ran along my spine.

How would I ever resist Jeffrey Hills?

4

JEFFREY

My throat closed. No air could come in and out of my lungs. I'd never meant to fall for my brother's best friend. Especially considering I was pretty sure my brother had feelings for her too. I'd known Dahlia Ellis my entire life. I used to cheer them on when they were just kids singing songs to us in her backyard. For as long as I remembered, I considered her a little sister.

Not anymore.

No matter how I tried to bury my feelings and stay away from her, I failed. Dahlia occupied all my thoughts. Even at school, I became a fool every time I caught sight of her or heard her laughter in the hallway.

Nobody knew about my crush. Not even my friends. It'd been going on for quite some time but had intensified in the last few months. So much that I was miserable the days we didn't cross paths. I tried to ignore my soaring feelings. I really did.

Two years ago, I even dated Vanessa to forget about

Dahlia, but it backfired because she cheated on me, accusing me of not caring about her.

Lately, I noticed how Dahlia had been looking at me. With heat and a glint in her eyes.

Each time our eyes met, my heart either beat faster or jammed in my chest.

Somehow, I wished Carter would have taken much longer to come back home tonight. For once, I had Dahlia all to myself, and I wasn't ready to give her back. Not that she belonged to Carter. Dahlia belonged to nobody. But deep inside me, I wished she'd belonged to me. That she'd be all mine. *Be mine and screw everybody else*, I wanted to tell her.

Last night, in the dark, unable to fall asleep, I wondered if what I felt for Dahlia could perhaps be called love. Did being in love make you feel like your heart could explode the moment the other person walked into a room? Because that's how it was with her. The moment she entered a room, she sucked all the oxygen from it. My skin itched, my lungs idled, my pulse picked up. Dahlia owned parts of my heart I didn't even know existed before they beat for her, and she had no clue about it.

My eyes stayed glued to her back as she followed Carter in the hallway. Now that she was gone, I could still smell her perfume all over my room. A floral mix I could get drunk on.

I missed her presence the minute she disappeared from my line of vision, leaving me without any viable air to breathe.

Why did I feel so lonely right now?

Except for Carter, I'd never felt so at ease with any other human being before.

Everything about Dahlia fascinated me. Her hair the color

of blazing flames. Her contagious smile. The way she fidgeted with her hands when she was nervous. Her moss-green eyes clouding when she was lost in her thoughts. The pale freckles sprinkled over her nose and cheeks that darkened during summer and that I wished I could trace over with my finger.

"Hey, guys, do you mind if I listen to you practice?" I asked as I slumped on the ugly brown sofa in our garage, which Dahlia had covered with a glittery pink blanket years ago to give it a second life.

I wanted to be close to her—breathe her air, bask in her energy—so I invaded their rehearsal space.

"Okay, I've made some changes. What do you think about this version?" Carter asked as he played two different intros for the newest song he composed. My brother was a guitar genius. Or prodigy, as Dad often said. When he was four, he grabbed a guitar in a music shop on Main Street and started playing like he'd been taking lessons for years. Then he taught Dahlia. And tried to teach me too, but it ended up being a disaster. I had no rhythm nor "guitar-fingers," as Carter told me once.

Music was something he shared with Dahlia. What passion did Dahlia and I have in common? I sighed, none coming to my mind. What could we bond over? I scratched the side of my head, my brain rattling to find something. Why was it so important for me to find some-thing we both loved? I was making myself dizzy.

Dahlia stayed silent, not looking at me. Why was she ignoring me? I thought we were good earlier before Carter barged in.

My insides heated up, and I clenched my hands into fists.

My heart lost a chunk for every second Dahlia acted as if I didn't exist.

I leaned forward, propping my elbows on my bent knees, hiding my face with my hands.

"The second version," I said, answering Carter's question about his song, trying to infuse some pep into my words. "What about you, Dah?" I was hungry for her attention.

Carter and I both cocked our heads in her direction. Standing there, with the guitar in her hands and her jaw slack, Dahlia's gaze traveled between the two of us. She looked adorable in her purple top—her favorite color—and her black jeans with embroidered silver flowers on the back pockets. A bright crimson flush colored her cheeks. Her eyes flared. I bit my inner cheek to avoid smiling.

"I—I—Huh, sorry, I wasn't listening." Dahlia angled her face to look at my brother. "Can you play it again?"

Was Dahlia distracted because of me?

Carter played the part again, and Dahlia's thoughtful eyes sucked me in. She pursed her lips before biting her lower one. How I longed to nibble on her plump lip.

My body overheated. Every inch of me tensed. I rubbed the heels of my hands over my eyes, to dissipate the image. "I need to go, guys. I'll see you both later."

Did I nail the calm and composed tone?

Jumping to my feet, I hurried outside, craving some fresh air and needing a high dose of oxygen through my bloodstream to keep my brain going.

I fanned my hand before my face as my feet landed on the pavement.

I kicked the air, releasing the tension in the crotch of my pants. Even my body was sensitive to Dahlia Ellis's beauty and charm.

What was I supposed to do now?

I paced the driveway, talking to myself, urging my body to calm down.

My thoughts swirled back to her. Over and over. Her face was etched on my mind. Everywhere I looked, she appeared before my eyes. Her scent had left a permanent mark in my lungs. Everything smelled like her. And I was pretty sure if I tasted her lips, her flavor would linger on mine until the day I died.

With my fingers laced on my nape and my elbows opened wide on each side, I tilted my head, looking at the blue sky.

If rain poured on me, would it wash away all my dirty thoughts? Would it reset my senses?

I sighed. Nothing could be powerful enough to erase my crush. Dahlia Ellis lived in my heart. She existed under my skin. Her essence was in my soul, her touch engraved on mine. My eyes yearned to see her; my arms belonged around her. We fitted, she and I, like the halves of a whole. Every time we brushed against one another, it validated what I already knew deep inside me. I loved her.

My heart ached. My spine tingled. I darted my tongue out to moisten my dry lips.

I breathed out, and peace settled inside me. My body relaxed. Sorta.

Not in the mood to face either Carter or Dahlia again tonight, I climbed into my truck and drove away.

I dialed my friend, Brendan. "Hey, man. Meet me at Milwaukee Park in fifteen. Bring a football or something, I need to vent."

I hung up and called another number.

"Hey, Mom. I won't make it to dinner. Don't wait for me, I'm going out."

"Is everything all right, Jeffrey?"

"Yeah. Everything is perfectly fine."

Bullshit. Nothing was fine. How long could I survive this?

———

Two weeks later

A soft knock on my door startled me. I raised my eyes from my computer screen and pivoted in my chair. Carter appeared in the doorway.

"Hey, can I come in?"

"Sure," I said, forcing my brooding away. "How are things going?"

"Great. Is something wrong? You're never home, and it's like you're avoiding me. Did I do anything to piss you off?"

I motioned for Carter to sit on my bed. I missed my brother. We barely ever fought. We'd always been like twins, born three years apart. I hated the idea he thought I was upset with him. All I wanted was to stay as far away as possible from him and Dahlia. For all our sakes.

"Got a lot on my mind. I haven't picked a college yet, and Mom is on my back about it. She wants me to get a college education before enlisting or doing whatever else I'm supposed to do."

"What do you want to do?"

"I don't know. Maybe getting away from here is the right thing to do." I dropped my head on my desk with a loud thud.

"It can't be that hard. Pick a college, get Mom and Dad off your back, then take the time to decide."

"Maybe you're right. I'm sorry I've been distant."

Concern took over Carter's eyes. "Are you serious about the Army stuff, though? I'm not sure it suits you."

I lifted my head from my desk and shrugged. "Yes. No. I'm not sure either. Maybe I could do some good, you know? Change the world or something. It's not really about the Army, but more about helping people who might need it. Be part of something—"

Before my brother could say another word, I rose to my feet and grabbed him in a headlock. He let out a laugh and started wrestling me. We fell on the bed, both of us holding tight to each other. Carter had shot up over four inches in the last year. He now neared the six-foot-five mark. I was three inches shorter but broader than him, so it compensated for my lack of height.

"I'll drive you to the restaurant on Saturday night. Tell Dahlia she can come along if she wants."

My brother let go of me. "Thanks, man. I appreciate it. You should apply to be our road manager. I'm sure you'd be good at it. I might even get you a 'number one fan' title ribbon to wear to every show. Something bright pink with glitter and flashing lights."

"You're so stupid," I said, unable to stop laughing. My younger brother had a knack for improving my mood. "How about I treat you to burgers instead?"

"With milkshake and Cajun fries?"

"I wouldn't offer anything less," I said with a wink.

"Count me in. I'll meet you downstairs in fifteen."

Carter exited my room, and I exhaled all the angst filling my lungs.

Thirty minutes later, we were seated in a booth at the back of Bryce's Burgers. The place was filled with young families and teenagers. The walls were painted in some royal shade of blue, and the ceiling was a light shade of silver. Surfboards—which didn't make sense in the middle of Tennessee—were hung on the walls. Palm trees with wrapped-around lights framed the entrance.

The staff behind the counter wore colorful leis and bright red shirts with exotic birds on them. The place looked festive. No country music or a Southern feeling here. It looked straight from 1980s California instead. Our parents had been bringing Carter and me here since we were kids. It was one of our favorite spots in town.

"So, who are you taking to prom?" Carter asked, pushing a handful of fries inside his mouth, chewing as he spoke.

"Man, you're gross."

"Any name? I heard there were at least ten girls who asked you to go with them already. Did you pick one?"

I shook my head. "There's only one girl I want to ask to prom. But I'm not sure she'll agree to be my date."

"Who is she? Anyone I know?"

I shrugged. "It doesn't matter. I won't ask her."

"Since when do you chicken out?"

I shrugged again, taking a huge bite of my burger to avoid answering my brother's twenty questions.

"C'mon, Jeff. Don't be a chickenshit. Grow some balls. What's the worst that can happen? Being rejected? So what? Girls are lining up to go with you. It's not like you'll end up going alone."

I swallowed the remnants of my burger bite and washed it up with a sip of my Coke. "I'm not even sure I wanna go. So, it doesn't really matter."

"You can't skip all the traditions, man. You've already bailed on Homecoming and Winter Formal. You know Mom is dying to buy you a suit and take embarrassing pictures of you and your date, right?"

I threw pieces of fries at him. As my reply.

"Anyway, I don't think I'm on this girl's radar." No way I'd tell him the truth.

Carter fished a quarter from his pocket and smirked. Damn it. I knew what was coming, and I clutched the edge of the table with all my strength. This wouldn't end well. I could already tell. "You asked for it. I'll take the matter into my own hands. Brace yourself, big brother—destiny will decide. Head, you're asking this mystery girl. Tail, you bail on prom or pick a girl from your fan club. You should've asked for my help sooner. I'm a miracle maker, and I'll fix your prom problems."

I cringed as my brother flicked the coin. I stopped breathing as the coin flipped in the air. The two seconds it took Carter to catch it back felt like forever. My brother opened his mouth, and my chest tightened. Spots danced in my vision.

"Head. The coin has decided. You ask her. I'll give you two days to man up and get your head out of your ass." He lifted one finger. "And I'll need a full report in forty-eight hours. Don't let me down, brother."

I sucked in a breath. Carter had no idea how messy this would turn out to be. What did I get myself into?

I pushed my plate away, not hungry anymore. I eyed Carter sideways. Would I ever be able to steal the girl he was obsessed with from him? I doubted Dahlia was in love with my brother. Sure, she cared for him. A lot.

But from the way she chewed on her full bottom lip every time I was around, and how her eyes lit up whenever we were in the same room, I was pretty sure Dahlia cared for me too. More than I'd ever felt possible. My pulse sprinted just at the thought of it.

Fire stirred inside me. I pressed a palm to my chest, easing the pain.

Carter didn't need to have his heart broken. Not by his big brother. And his best friend.

He trusted me.

Fuck.

"Promise me, you'll ask this girl to prom. No matter what."

I nodded. My insides turned to stone. My stomach churned. "I will."

The back of my throat filled with acid. And shame.

———

My last two nights hadn't been restful. Both times, I'd tossed and turned for hours. Now I looked like shit. Great. I caught my reflection in the bathroom mirror. Bags under my eyes, dried lips from biting on them, last night's rumpled T-shirt still on.

For the last fifteen minutes, I'd been pacing my bedroom. If I continued, I'd dig a tunnel to the kitchen below. I tugged at the roots of my hair. My heart beat so fast I thought I'd die from a heart attack. Carter's two-day deadline expired today.

He wouldn't miss a chance to remind me this morning before we left for school that my time was up and that I needed to grow some balls.

"Big furry balls," as he said last night. Troubling. My brother had a gift for etching gross images into my mind.

I went downstairs, trying to keep a low profile. Yeah, who was I kidding? Carter was waiting for me in the kitchen with his obnoxious smirk on and his wild mass of dark wavy hair falling over his face.

"Good morning, sunshine," he greeted as I joined him. "Sleep well?" He studied me. "Shit, what happened? Did you sleep on a bed of nails?"

I flipped him the finger. "Fuck you, man."

"This girl kept you up all night? You're lucky she isn't your girlfriend, or you wouldn't sleep for the rest of your life by the looks of you."

"Go to hell."

"Oh, someone is a little sensitive this morning. Get

your groove back on, *Jeffy*. Today is the day you're becoming a man. You haven't asked any girl out since Vanessa. Two years ago."

"So what?"

"Vanessa wasn't the fastest car in the left lane, if you catch my quip."

"Shut up, man. You're not helping. It's seven in the morning, for God's sake." I dragged my hands over my face.

"You're better off without her. I'm glad she cheated on you. Well, not glad, but— Anyway, you're better off."

I sighed and threw a dishcloth at him. Straight in the chest. "Just stop talking for once." My brother raised his hands in surrender.

"Fine. But don't be a chicken today, big bro. You have to fulfill your destiny," he said as he gulped orange juice straight from the carton. "The coin decided."

"Yeah," I said with a groan. I raked my fingers through my hair.

"You made a promise."

"I know." My tone was harsh. Carter stared at me with arched brows.

"Don't overthink it, Jeff. It's just prom, not a marriage proposal. Your face is grayish. If I didn't know you better, I'd think you're gonna barf your breakfast in the next minute."

I pushed him as we crossed paths in the hallway.

"Don't get on my nerves. I'm not in the mood."

"Whatever you say," Carter said, a wide grin lighting up his face and a glint in his eyes. He yelled, "Mom," at the top of his lungs. "Jeff's in lo—" I punched him in the stomach so that he'd keep his stupid mouth shut.

Carter bent over and rubbed his midsection with one hand, his smirk reaching his eyes. "No need to kill me over this, bro. Whoever the chick is, she'd be lucky to go to prom with you."

I clenched my hands in my pockets and lowered my head, my chin pressed against my chest. "Thanks, man." I swallowed hard. If only he knew. In just a few hours, I'd be the one rubbing that goofy smile off his face. Great. Just great.

———

After school, I loitered on my way back home. In desperate need to release the built-up energy inside me this morning, I ran to school. I knew the moment my feet would land on the kitchen floor, Carter would be all over me about asking that girl to prom. I stopped by Bryce's to grab a strawberry milkshake. It was my go-to comfort food. Or drink. Whatever.

I strolled through Milwaukee Park, taking the detour around the large grassy patch that hosted a soccer field instead of the straight-through path leading to our street. I contoured the field where I played touch football with Brendan and a bunch of guys from school every weekend during summer break.

It was a beautiful day, and the sun, still shining high, erased some of my angst. Seated on a bench, I watched a mother duck and her three ducklings playing and diving under the water. The sight of them, so clueless about everything else in the world, brought a small smile to my lips.

But it didn't last long.

On my left, my eyes caught a movement, and I swiveled my head in that direction. A girl, about twelve or thirteen years old, with long, wavy red hair was running after a beagle on a leash. The image of her red—hot as scorching lava—hair, flowing around her face acted like a clamp around my heart.

I tilted my head back and cursed.

Not thirsty anymore, I threw my milkshake into the nearest trashcan and ambled toward my house, my back curved forward, my hands deep in my pockets, the weight of the world sitting on my shoulders.

I made a promise to Carter, and I would honor it. And I would deal with the consequences afterward. Not smart. But was there a right way to do this? I was done being miserable. And I was confident Dahlia felt something for me too.

I entered the house from the back door. The chatter coming from the kitchen stopped me in my tracks. Dahlia's clear as crystal laughter made my heart beat faster. It sent a shot of adrenaline through my bloodstream.

On my tiptoes, I ventured upstairs without a sound but failed to make it further up when my mom noticed me from where she stood.

"Hey, Jeffrey, you're home. Are you joining us for dinner?"

I cringed. This was the moment.

I could make it awkward or just hold my chin up, rip the Band-Aid off, and stop worrying about it.

"Sure, I'll be there in a sec."

Before Carter could say something, I climbed the remaining stairs two by two. In my room, I picked a new T-shirt, a steel-blue one that I knew made my eyes look more vibrant—Mom had told me many times—and hurried to the bathroom. I washed my armpits and applied a fresh coat of deodorant, brushed my teeth, and put the clean tee on.

"You can do this, man. Don't be a chicken. Go down there, ask her, and look confident. Be sure of yourself."

I closed my eyes, exhaled all the air in my lungs, and whispered a hasty prayer she'd say yes and that my brother would forgive me.

I wasn't asking Dahlia out—not yet, at least—just to prom. I'd use the friendship card if it came to it.

With steady steps and a straight back, I made it to the kitchen, doing my best to hide the cluster of mixed emotions rumbling inside me.

Dahlia sat at the counter, chopping vegetables for dinner, as Mom stood by the stove, stirring tomato sauce.

Carter was busy with math homework, sitting next to her.

And Dad was nowhere to be seen.

One less spectator to witness what could be an epic rejection.

I cleared my throat. Carter's eyes lifted to meet mine. I offered him a tight-lipped smile, braced myself, and puffed my chest out.

"Hey, Dah. I've been wanting to ask you something for a while now." She glanced at me, her green eyes drawing me in. My heart almost tipped over in my chest. I could do this. "Would you go to prom with me?"

A guttural sound tumbled out of Carter's mouth, and his eyes flared. Could he pop an eyeball?

His face turned a dark shade of red.

He dropped the pencil he was holding, and his hands balled into fists at his sides.

I swallowed hard.

Mom gasped as she turned on her heels to watch the scene.

The beating of my heart and my own gasps were all I could hear.

Dahlia raised her eyes. Our gazes collided. She parted her lips to say something, and a dark pink flush covered her cheeks. The throbbing pulse in her neck matched mine.

Her head turned. Her eyes found Carter's.

They exchanged one of their silent stares that nobody understood but them.

I held my breath, each passing second bringing me closer to fainting from lack of oxygen to my brain.

5

DAHLIA

My heart bounced in my chest. I sucked in a breath, but it didn't go through. A high-pitched gasp mixed with a cough tumbled out instead.

Was my face firetruck red?

I slid my shaky hands under my thighs.

Jeff asked me to be his prom date.

Jeff asked me to be his prom date.

Jeff asked me to be his prom date.

Would repeating it over and over make it sound as if it was no big deal? Would it make it sound real?

Jeff had a dozen girls at school—all tall, pretty, and older than me—waiting for him to ask them.

But he asked me. Me. Dahlia Ellis, fifteen-year-old freshman, best friend to his younger brother.

I blinked. And blinked again.

I swallowed, trying to bring moisture back to my mouth.

My lungs burned. When did I stop breathing?

A soft thud on my left startled me.

My eyes landed on Carter, who I forgot was still seated next to me. He gave me a nod—so small most people wouldn't have noticed it—and curled his spine forward. His eyes bled with hurt. And pain. His shoulders drooped in defeat. My heart broke into tiny pieces and scattered in my chest. I exhaled.

My eyes traveled to Jeff. Looking hot in his blue shirt with short, dark, tousled hair and eyes full of expectation.

The dimples in his cheeks, as he offered me a shy, lopsided smile, fused the pieces of my heart back together. One by one. Jeff hooked his thumbs into his jeans and shrugged. There was so much hope in his eyes that I couldn't look away.

All my senses heightened. My ears caught Jeff's small intake of breath. The whole marching band played in my chest. And I felt every note. My skin tingled. I parted my lips to gulp as much air as possible, but all that came through was Jeff's sandalwood and cinnamon scent. So strong and intoxicating, I was lightheaded.

For a moment, I forgot all about Carter and his mama watching us.

My heart switched from bouncing to dancing inside my chest.

"So?"

Jeff bit his lower lip and stared at me with a gleam I'd never seen before.

When did I become mute?

This.

This was what I'd been wishing for, in secret, for weeks now. Every single time I wrote "Dahlia Hills" in my notebook.

I got up from my seat and approached Jeff on trembling legs. Raising my gaze to his, I wound my arms around his neck, and Jeff picked me up.

With my eyes swimming in his, I found my voice.

"I'd like to. Very much." His grin spread all over his face. Now feeling like an imposter, I asked, "Are you sure you want to take me?"

Jeff bobbed his head. Butterflies took flight in my stomach. "Yeah. I do. So, is it a yes?"

I nodded a little too fast, unable to erase that silly smile from my face.

Our eyes drank each other in for a long minute, neither of us saying anything else. I could see the stars in Jeff's eyes. Could he see the sparks in mine? Could he tell how happy I was right now?

Without releasing my waist, Jeff put me down on my feet. My cheeks felt so warm, I could have burned down the house with the fire blazing inside me.

Mrs. Hills clapped her hands in front of her, and I snapped out of my trance.

"This is wonderful," she said. "You two will make an adorable couple. Your mama will be so excited, Dahlia." She pivoted until she faced Carter, sitting still, his math homework long forgotten. "Carter, set the table. Dinner will be ready in five minutes." Then she faced Jeff and me. "You two make me so proud. I can't wait to see you all dressed up." Mrs. Hills leaned forward, rose to her tiptoes, and dropped a kiss on her oldest son's cheek. Then she grabbed my upper arms and pulled me into a hug. "You'll make my boy happy, Dahlia," she whispered in my ear. "I just know it."

Without another word, she got back to her sauce simmering on the stove.

I watched Carter, a crestfallen expression clouding his face.

Freshly glued-together pieces of my heart fell one by one.

Was Carter's mama clueless about his feelings for me, or did she not care?

My happiness crumbled as sadness shadowed my best friend's now red-rimmed eyes.

I inched closer to him and placed my hand on his forearm. Carter tensed then relaxed.

A deep sigh escaped his lips. He placed his hand over mine and raised his gaze to me, helpless in his pain. Tears pooled in both our eyes as we acknowledged our love and the doings of our heart. Both of us were helpless in whom it chose. And now we would have to live with the repercussions.

I closed my eyes as rivulets made their way down my cheeks. Carter's did too. Only Jeff was the silent witness to the bond that broke and reformed with this changed equation between us.

"Hey," I said softly. Carter nodded, understanding what I couldn't say aloud.

He forced a smile on his lips. "I'm glad for you two. I was the one who wanted Jeff to ask the girl he liked to prom. I just didn't know it would be you."

The words died in my mouth. Whichever Hills brother I chose, the other would be left devastated. It was an impossible situation.

A wildfire erupted inside me, one big enough to ravage an entire forest.

"I'm sorry, Cart. I shouldn't have said yes so quickly. Jeff should've asked me in private, and we should've talked about this. The three of us. I don't want things to be weird between us. You'll always be my best friend. Forever. It changes nothing." I traced a cross over my heart. "It's only prom, okay? We won't make a big deal out of it. I promise." Carter hung his head low. "We can talk after dinner."

My best friend's eyes found mine. "No. No need to

hear all about that stupid glittery chiffon dress you'll want to wear." He made a gagging sound and winked. I smiled, knowing how much that cost him. Our friendship was safe. For now.

"Thanks," I said as I hugged him. Carter hugged me back. "And yes, I'll even try on the ugliest dress we find at the store just for your sake. And I might even let you take a picture if you promise to not laugh when you see me in it." Carter shook his head, but a small smile peeked at the corner of his lips. I warmed up at the sight of it. With both hands, I pulled him by the collar, and when he leaned in, I kissed his cheek. "You're the best." I let go of my friend and lifted the pile of plates and silverware Mrs. Hills had placed on the kitchen island and took it upon myself to set the table.

Dinner lasted forever. Sitting next to Jeff, I did my best to avoid looking at him the entire time, his closeness powerful enough to ignite fireworks inside me.

I focused all my attention on my best friend. No way would my going to prom with his brother impact our friendship. I'd never let it happen. My feet found Carter's under the table, and the same way we'd always done since we were kids, we entangled them together. And as always, it soothed every doubt inside me. Every nagging voice. Every fear.

"What was the bet Phoenix made during gym class today?" I asked, keeping the conversation as far away from prom as possible.

Carter choked on a piece of bread and sipped on his water.

"That?" His eyes lit up. "You should've seen it. It was the worst. He bet he'd climb the rope, you know, the one with the knots, in less than a minute, using only his arms. He failed. Someone put itching powder in his shirt. After like three knots, Phen dropped to the ground and rolled around, scratching like a dog with fleas. It was hilarious. Anyway, since he lost, he has to cross the field tomorrow at practice, wearing a neon-pink bikini bottom. Coach will bench him for sure, but it'll be priceless. You can't miss it. You should watch it with me from the bleachers."

Jeff, on my left side, snickered.

"Oh, that's terrible. I wouldn't miss it for the world. Count me in."

My laughter died in my throat when Jeff's hand gripped mine under the table. He laced our fingers together, and my heart stopped.

I pinched my lips together, making sure Carter wouldn't notice me shifting in my seat.

Jeff's hand, all large, soft, and warm, made me giddy.

Tension released from my shoulders as I exhaled.

From that moment on, I knew it in my heart.

My hand belonged in Jeff Hills's hand.

———

"You're sure this is a good fit on me?" I asked Addison as she zipped my gown, a tulle steel-blue A-line dress with gems sewed to the bodice. It matched Jeff's buttoned-up shirt. This shade of blue was my favorite color on him, and it also looked fabulous with my copper hair. My girlfriend —a fanatic for anything beauty-related, thanks to her mama owning a beauty salon—had applied dark gray glittery shadow to my eyelids and a coat of black mascara to my lashes. She'd curled my hair and tied it in a complicated half updo, leaving a few strands loose around my face.

"Are you crazy, Dah? You look like a princess. Jeff will

go crazy when he sees you. Don't be surprised if the heat between you two goes through the roof."

"I don't want him to think I tried too hard." I sighed. Would Jeff's friends treat me like I belonged? A dozen knots tied my stomach at the thought they would all see me as a kid playing grown-up for a night.

"Dah, it was all him. He chose you. And I'm sure Jeff Hills can hold up his end if anybody says anything. Don't worry about it. Neither of the Hills brothers would ever do anything to hurt you or your feelings."

"Still—"

"No still, Dah. Put a smile on your face and enjoy your night. All the girls will wish they were you. They would all want to be on his arm tonight. Remember he chose you."

"I—"

A soft knock on the door interrupted us.

Carter peeked inside my bedroom. His lips parted. His eyes rounded.

"Wow, you look—you look—"

My mouth went dry. "That bad, huh?"

"You're kidding? You look perfect." I spun around once Addison finished zipping me up.

"You're sure?"

His Adam's apple bobbed. He gave me a slow once-over.

"Dah, you're beautiful." Our eyes met, and I noticed a shadow clouding his irises. We'd talked about prom countless times over the last two months, and Carter promised he was okay with me going with his brother. But deep down, I knew he hid the truth from me. I could read it in his eyes every time he stared my way and thought I wasn't aware.

It crushed my heart a little more each time.

But then, Jeff's gaze would land on me, and I'd forget

everything else. His eyes would darken. He'd rub the back of his neck. Look away for a second and shake his legs—I believed to relieve the discomfort growing between them. Yeah, I noticed. Deep in my core, I knew I'd made the right choice.

Carter cleared his throat. "I'm here to escort you home. I volunteered to be the one walking you over." Carter offered me his hand, and I held on to it like a lifeline. Just his touch was enough to calm my pounding heart.

"I need to get going anyway," Addison said. She neared me and pulled me into a hug. "Have fun tonight, girlfriend. And call me tomorrow morning."

"I will." My friend left, and I found myself alone with Carter.

I wiped the corners of my eyes with my fingertips, trying not to mess up my makeup.

Carter inched closer, worry in his eyes. "You okay?"

"Yep. Thanks for being here for me. I'm not sad, just overwhelmed." Carter bowed his head and led me away.

At the top of the staircase, I halted, afraid I'd trip over my gown. Carter saw my hesitation because he lifted the back of my dress and gripped my elbow as we made it downstairs.

"Nice boots," he said with a wink. I poked his arm with my finger.

Tonight, I wore cowboy boots instead of heels—which I'd never worn before—to avoid the risk of breaking one of my ankles and humiliating myself.

Carter and I paraded down the street as we walked to his house. Mrs. Canterbury, our old neighbor, waved at us from the white wooden swing on her front porch.

"You look good, kids," she said.

"Thanks, Mrs. Canterbury," both Carter and I said at the same time.

"I need to warn you, Dah. Mom is going crazy in there. I came to get you to give you a heads-up. Everything Jeff-related is always the highlights of her days, so you can imagine the setup." Carter's tone turned sour. "Jeff can do no wrong. I'm sure she's already planning your wedding to him." I stopped in my tracks and turned to face my best friend. Hurt flashed in his eyes, darker tonight. I grabbed his hands in mine and laced our fingers together.

"I know it seems unfair, but your mama loves you. She just has a weird way of showing it sometimes. And I think she has no idea how to relate to your music. I heard her the other day, talking to my mama, and she couldn't stop praising how smart you were."

Carter blinked back what I believed were tears. Hand in hand, we made it to his house. On the front porch, I rose to my tiptoes, and my lips grazed his cheek.

"Thanks for warning me. And for walking me over. Please don't hide in your room just yet because I want pictures with you, okay?"

Carter nodded, and we exchanged a smile.

"Ready?"

I filled my lungs and tightened my grip on his hand.

"Let's do this."

One hour later, my ass landed on the passenger seat of Jeff's truck, and I sighed. Jeff was driving us tonight, and I was grateful he did. I needed to breathe away from everybody else as we escaped the camera madness going on in his house. Both our mamas snapped an infinite number of pictures of us. Inside. Outside in the backyard. On the front lawn. By the fireplace. In his bedroom, faking getting ready together.

Mama took pictures of Carter and me, and some of Carter, Jeff, and I together. We tried secret spies poses with our hands folded together as handguns, and another where the guys threw a football as I stood between them, in my gown, my arms crossed over my chest, with a pout.

I should frame the last one we took. Mama showed it to me before we left, and I couldn't look away. It was etched on my mind.

It was a shot of us three in the garage. Carter and I playing one of our songs as Jeff, in a suit with a loosened tie, his arms spread on either side of the backrest of the sofa, watched us. Watched me. My throat clenched at the memory of how I traced his handsome face with the pad of my forefinger over the camera screen.

"You okay?" Jeff asked after he helped me settle my gown, closed the door behind me, and circled his truck to get in, pulling me out of my daydream.

"Yeah. I'm glad we escaped the circus, though."

"Me too." Jeff leaned over the console between our seats. "Can I tell you something now that we're alone?"

Warmth pooled in my cheeks. My heart hammered in my chest. I wiggled my toes to get rid of the tingles that had started in my limbs. Why was it that every time Jeff talked to me, I felt I was close to collapse?

"You look beautiful." A small flush crept over Jeff's shaved face. Tonight, he wore a black suit over his steel-blue shirt and a black tie. He'd gelled his short hair in spikes. A glint lit up his face. "Can I do something?" My heart threatened to explode. My pulse deafened me. I bobbed my head.

Jeff tipped my chin with his finger and leaned closer. His lips brushed mine, and I thought my chest would burst open. Flutters filled me. I closed my eyes and swallowed hard. When I re-opened them, Jeff's face was an inch from mine. He was panting. I lost myself in his gaze; I could see the glow in it. The hair on my arms stood on end, and his lips found mine again. This time he kissed me—a real kiss.

A flood of heat rippled through me, making prom seem not so important anymore. Jeff's lips were everything I ever wished they'd be. Soft. Warm. Experienced. Mine.

He pulled back and started the engine. "I've been dying to do this for so long."

I failed at holding back the smile taking my face hostage.

"Please. Don't wait that long next time." His face snapped in my direction. Jeff glanced at me with what I would define as a mix of longing, lust, and surprise. My hand flew to my mouth. I couldn't believe I said that out loud. But then my date grinned, and the tension in my upper back vanished. He intertwined our fingers together and rested our joined hands in my lap.

His warmth traveled through me, lighting up every cell, every pore.

My eyes lingered on Jeff's lips, and I traced mine with my finger, wishing we could kiss all night. Hoping the feeling would never wash away.

Shivers moved along my spine, igniting my body.

Addi would freak out when I tell her about it.

My heart filled my chest to the brim. Nothing could temper my happiness tonight.

We entered the school gym, transformed into an enchanted garden—the prom theme. Green tablecloths, looking like moss, covered the tables. A path lined with lanterns showed the way to the photo booth. All over the room, there were fake bushes trimmed into swans, and garden-ball lamps hung from the ceiling, giving the place a touch of magic.

I took in everything in awe. "Wow, this is beautiful." Jeff's hands found mine.

We stared at each other for a beat, the magnetic pull between us stronger than it had ever been before.

He raked his fingers through his hair, messing it up.

I turned around to face him, a small smile curving my lips. "Here. Let me."

I rose to the tips of my toes, and in the same way I'd always done with Carter, I combed Jeff's hair back in place with my fingers. This time the feelings were different. My breath caught in my lungs. Warm jitters ran through me. Jeff stopped breathing too. He cradled my face with his hands, his irises darkening. His stare traveled between my eyes and lips.

"Not here," I said, my voice uneven. Jeff lowered his head and nodded. I wouldn't risk anyone taking a picture of us and Carter seeing it. I wasn't ready for this.

I gripped the lapel of his jacket, finding my balance. My knees wobbled, and with his hands clutching my waist, Jeff held me up.

My lips quivered.

They were dying to be kissed again. Just once more.

Jeff blew out a long breath and cleared his throat. "Let's go. I want to dance with you." Never letting go of his hand, I followed him to the dance floor.

The night passed in a blur. Jeff and I were in our own little bubble. We spent too much time dancing, the need to be in each other's arms growing bigger and stronger with each passing hour.

When we pulled into my driveway, something deflated inside me. I wasn't ready for the night to end.

"I'll walk you to your door," Jeff said, his voice husky. It sent shivers to my core. I curled my hand around his nape and pulled him forward. When our lips touched, I came alive. His scent invaded my nostrils.

We broke apart, breathless.

"Carter can't know," I said, tears burning the back of

my eyes. "I'm not sure he'll be okay with this," I said, gesturing to the two of us with my free hand.

"I know. I don't want him to feel left out." Jeff let out a long breath. "But I'm having a hard time staying away from you, Princess. I know we shouldn't, but somehow, it feels right. So damn right." Goosebumps blossomed on my skin. My heart raced in my chest. Butterflies flew around in my tummy.

"Let's take it slow and see where it's going before saying anything, okay?" Pressing his forehead against mine, Jeff sighed.

"Yeah. But seeing you every day and not being able to kiss you will be the worst kind of torture." He wrapped his arms around my back, and I sank my head in his chest, the beating of his heart the only music I would ever need. "We won't go behind his back. It wouldn't be right. But we'll figure this out. Do you trust me?" I bobbed my head, still buried in his chest. Warm tears rolled down my cheeks. I wiped them off with my fingertips. "We'll give him time—"

I said nothing, fighting the sobs bubbling in my throat. Jeff leaned back and tilted my head with one finger.

"Hey, what's wrong? Talk to me."

"Do you think Carter will forgive us one day? I don't want to lose him. He's been my best friend forever. I love him. And I'd never do anything to hurt him."

"I know. He might be upset at first, but he loves us both, and we love him. I'm sure we can find a way to make it work." I heard him swallow. "I need to ask you something, though. Are you in love with my brother?"

I locked my eyes on Jeff's and shook my head. "No. I love him. I do. A lot. But I'm not in love with him, even if he's the most important person in my life. Other than—" A sob escaped my mouth and drowned my words.

Jeff dried my tears with his thumbs. "Don't cry, Princess. I feel hopeless when you're sad." I pressed my cheek against his warm palm. Our eyes met. Again. Like a force bigger than us was pulling us toward each other.

Jeff brought his mouth back on mine, his teeth toying with my shuddering bottom lip.

Once inside, after Jeff kissed me goodnight—half a dozen times—I leaned my back against the front door and let go of all the air lodged in my lungs. Mama turned on the light in the kitchen and neared me, her eyes full of concern.

"Sweetie, are you okay?" She closed the distance between us and enveloped me in a much-needed hug. Her hair, a darker shade of red than mine, tickled my face. I breathed her in. She smelled like cinnamon rolls. Had she been baking all night? Tears ran down my cheeks. Her scent reminded me of Jeff's.

With my face pressed against her chest, my head motioned yes. Then a no.

A long-buried sob exited my mouth.

"What's wrong?" I snorted, unable to tell her everything going on inside me. "Oh, baby. It's okay." She caressed my hair with her fingers. The same way she did when I was sad as a little girl.

"Mama—" My throat was dry, my mouth pasty.

"You love him?"

After a brief hesitation, trying to put words onto my feelings, I let out a throaty "Yes."

"And you're scared to break Carter's heart?"

I snorted and nodded again. How could Mama know so much about how troubled my heart was?

"It was meant to happen someday, sweetie. Those two boys are both head over heels in love with you. That much is obvious. But you can't be in love with both. As your mama, I know where your heart stands. And I also know Carter will be heartbroken. But when he sees you and Jeff together, one day he'll understand. You both are doing a poor job of hiding your attraction. Carter's feelings blind him. But soon he'll see what we all see. He'll come around. Give him some time to heal. Be gentle with his heart. It's precious. That boy wears his emotions like a second skin. That's why he's such a talented songwriter. Be there for him when he needs you and give him some space when he needs it, okay?"

"Yeah," I said, the soreness in my throat sharper. "Thanks, Mama."

She kissed the top of my head and kept her arms around me for a long time, rocking me to peace.

———

Two months later

"Have you seen Carter today?" I asked, sitting between Jeff's legs on a lounger in his backyard. "He's been MIA for the last three days."

Jeff brushed my hair over my shoulder. "He's in his room. Writing. Again."

I sighed.

Jeff and I started dating—officially—one month ago. After my sixteenth birthday. Things had never been the same between Carter and me since prom. Sure, we spent a lot of time together, hanging out and playing music, but his eyes often bore a sadness that wasn't there before. Jeff and I broke the news to him together. It turned out better than we expected, considering we were both crushing his heart. Carter never told me in words that he loved me, but I could feel it in my bones.

"I miss him."

"I do too, Princess. All his pain is transforming into amazing songs, though. So, it's not all bad. You'll have new original material by the end of summer. Music is his therapy. If he locks himself in his room for two more weeks, we'll stage an intervention, okay? Carter needs time to process the idea of us being together. I know my brother— he won't turn his back on us. When he's ready, we'll be here for him."

I sank into my boyfriend's arms, my own personal shelter. His lips trailed kisses on the back of my head. His arms fastened around me, and we stayed like that for a long time, just enjoying each other.

An idea crossed my mind, and I jumped to my feet. "Let's go pick burgers from Bryce's. It might cheer him up."

Jeff followed me. "Good idea, let me grab my truck keys."

When we came back with the greasy, smelly food, Carter couldn't resist and joined us for lunch. He had dark circles around his eyes, and his hair was a mess. Worse than usual. The three of us ate in silence. When Carter stood to go back to his room, I tugged at his arm and leaned closer. "I know you need your space right now, but I'm here if you wanna talk. Or hang out. Always and forever, okay?" Carter stared at me for long seconds, his hands stuffed in his pockets. "Don't shut me out, Cart. Please." Could he read my eyes and see everything I wanted to tell him? "I miss you."

Carter squeezed my upper arm. "I miss you too, Dah. We'll talk later, okay?"

Pieces of my heart went missing.

"Sure." Carter's lips connected with my forehead, and he disappeared upstairs.

That night, Jeff and I were on our way to a party, but halfway there, Jeff drove his pickup truck along an old dirty country lane and stopped once we were far away from the main road. We settled in the cargo bed, under the stars, stargazing just an excuse to make out.

His finger pads grazed the skin of my stomach underneath my loose white shirt, and he swallowed my moans as our mouths fused together.

Each time we kissed, my body yielded all its control to my very hot boyfriend. As if he possessed all the keys to unlock the doors to my soul.

Rising on my knees, I tied my hair in a knot and straddled him. Positioned over him, I felt his erection against my center. I pushed on his shoulders and leaned forward to deepen our kiss. My right hand ventured to his chest and lowered until I could cup the hard part of him over the fabric of his shorts.

"Hey, Princess, what are you doing?" Jeff asked, detaching our mouths, his voice low and rough. The sound of it lit up flames everywhere inside me. His dick twitched in my hand. Jeff exhaled through his mouth and closed his eyes. His heartbeat vibrated in every cell of mine. "Dah— Oh—Yes—No, you don't have to do that." His breathing quickened as I stroked him faster over his shorts. "Fuck." His eyes snapped open, and he studied me. With the high moon lighting up the night, I saw all the desire and restraint painted over his face. "Stop." I froze. And frowned.

"Uh, you don't like that?" Heat rose in me, and I blinked a few times.

"God no. You did nothing wrong, Princess. That's the problem. This feels too good. And I don't want to jizz in my pants. And we're not having sex; you're not ready."

I sighed. My cheeks must have turned ten shades darker.

"This is embarrassing," I said, wrinkling my nose.

Jeff squeezed my hands. "No. It felt amazing. Don't ever say that. You're perfect. I don't want us to rush things, but I love when you touch me."

He grinned, and I relaxed a little, my hand curving back around his thick erection.

"I know I'm not ready to sleep with you, but that doesn't mean we can't experiment, right?" I arched one brow, the way I knew he couldn't resist.

"God, I love you." When the words tumbled out, Jeff clamped his mouth shut, his eyes wide and face flushed.

My hands stopped their exploration.

"You love me?" Why did my voice sound so small? My heart hiccupped. All the racing thoughts and voices in my head died. Did I hear him right? Jeff loved me?

I tried to swallow but couldn't, my throat thick with emotions.

Jeff pushed himself up on his elbows, so our faces were inches apart. His eyes drew me in. "Yes. I do. I love you, Dahlia. I've loved you for a long time, Princess. But I didn't mean to blurt it out to you now. I wanted to wait for the right time. Not when you were playing with my dick."

Moisture filled my eyes.

"I don't care how you said it. I love you too. So damn much. Even if I'm not ready to have sex, it doesn't mean I can't make you feel good or that you can't touch me. Because I really, really want your hands on me."

I offered Jeff a shy smile, and without another word, I took his hands in mine and brought them to my breast. And just like that, I died a thousand times and got revived as many, as Jeff molded me to his palms.

"Fuck, Princess. I love you. You're all I'll ever want."

Our mouths found each other in a slow and steady rhythm. Our tongues danced together. My heart jumped out of my chest.

Jeff's hands traveled over my body, fueling all the flames inside me.

My hand dug into his boxer briefs, and for the very first time, I held his hard cock. His soft skin was the opposite of the hardness of his length. Jeff steadied his breathing as I pumped him and rubbed the pad of my thumb over the moist tip.

His hips buckled from the bottom of the cargo bed, and he stopped me.

"Enough, Princess." Jeff took a series of deep breaths.

I shook my head, looking straight into his glossy dark eyes.

"Let me finish." He tried to argue, but I worked him faster so he couldn't get a word out.

Jeff groaned. Something deep and primal. Seconds later, his hot thick cum flowed over my hand.

We stared at each other, neither of us able to form words, our love sealed in the most intimate way.

Once his breathing went back to normal, Jeff removed his black boxer briefs, and we used it to wipe ourselves clean.

"Princess, when you're ready, I'll be the one making you feel good." His lips found mine, and I dissolved in his mouth, the heat between us about to incinerate the entire town.

We kissed until our lips swelled. Until we were both breathless. Until my nipples were so stiff, they became too sensitive to be touched.

"Do you love me for real?" I asked. I wanted to fan myself. Did I have a stupid grin pasted on? My face heated up just at the thought of what we did. In the last hour, I became a woman. In so many ways.

Jeff pulled me into his arms and dropped a kiss on the tip of my nose. "I do. So much." Under the starry sky, we cuddled for hours, ditching the party, neither of us ready to go home.

———

A month later

My eyes brimmed with tears. My hands found my chest, thinking it'd be ripped apart. Could it? I had no idea. Never in my life did I have to say goodbye to someone. And now, standing in his room, nestled in his arms, his scent filling each cell of my body and my soul, I was doing it for the first time.

"Don't be sad, Princess," Jeff said as he tightened his grip around me. "I'll be back every few days. And we'll talk all the time."

I snorted. "I know. It doesn't make it easier, though."

Jeff cupped my cheeks and wiped my tears off. We stared into each other's depths. "It's just college, Dah. Not the other side of the world."

I tried to smile, but it fell flat. Who knew love could be that painful? Was this how Carter felt when he learned about me and Jeff dating? For his sake, I hoped not. Here I was, crying my weight in tears, and we weren't even breaking up. Just living in different cities. I was being silly.

"You'll be surrounded by girls older and smarter than me."

"Don't, Princess. Don't go there. It's you and me."

Our lips brushed, and I lost touch with everything

around me. Until Carter broke us apart, sliding between our entangled bodies with a cocky smirk.

I stepped back, and Jeff let go of me.

"Thought you left without saying goodbye, big bro."

Jeff rolled his eyes. "Never. I would've never heard the end of it."

Carter wrapped his arms around my shoulders, his cocky grin still on. "Stop breaking my best friend's heart, man. That's not cool. Just leave already. We'll be fine on our own." I backhanded Carter's chest but ended up smiling. Despite myself.

Jeff gave us a pointed look. "Now that I think of it, I'm not sure I like the idea."

I pushed Carter away and pressed Jeff's chest with both hands. "Forget Cart. He's desperate to keep you here with him. He's just not brave enough to tell you himself."

Carter burst into a fit of laughter. "Stop reading my mind, Dah. Anyway, you're wrong. I can't wait to have all of this to myself," he said, motioning his hand around. "I'll make this room my kingdom. Yeah, sounds about perfect."

Jeff moved me to the side and gripped Carter into a headlock.

I sighed. These two.

While they busied themselves wrestling, I went to Jeff's truck outside and placed one of his T-shirts, that I'd sprayed with my perfume, in his suitcase.

Carter and Jeff joined me minutes later, their faces flushed and their sibling spark fully on.

Jeff pulled his brother into a hug before pushing him. "Okay, bro. Gimme some time with my girl. I love you. Don't be stupid because I won't be there to watch over you. And keep an eye on Dah for me."

Carter clapped his brother's shoulder. "You got it."

Jeff pulled him into another hug before my best friend sauntered toward the house.

We both watched Carter as he disappeared inside.

"You know he's still hurting, right? I can see it in his eyes. His happy attitude is just a front," I said once he shut the door behind him.

Jeff sighed. "Yeah." He scratched the back of his neck. "I'm hoping with me gone, he'll get his groove back. I hate seeing him like this. Wait until he plays his new song. I heard it last night. It's fucking sad."

I balanced on my heels, my thumbs hooked to my denim skirt pockets.

"You think he'll get over it someday?"

"Yeah. He will. It'll be good for you two to spend more time together." I swallowed the boulder growing in my throat.

"I hope so. I miss him. And I'll miss you."

"I know. Now, come here, you," Jeff said, closing the gap between us. Like two magnets, we gravitated into each other's arms. "Miss me. But not too much, okay?"

"I'll try. Please be safe."

We hugged one last time before Jeff climbed into his truck.

He rolled his window down as he pulled out of the driveway. "I'll call you when I get there. I love you."

Hugging myself, I waved at him, not even bothering to wipe my tears off as a chunk of my heart drove away with the boy I loved.

6

DAHLIA

Three days later

Carter strummed his guitar, singing the last verse of his new song. Shivers ran through me. "I love it," I said. "You wrote this in one night? You know you're amazing, right?" Carter's smile widened. Pride radiated from him.

He shrugged. "Inspiration has been pouring out these last few weeks. I just can't stop writing. The other night I woke up five times to take notes because I was afraid I'd forget my ideas by the morning."

"I'm glad we're having a forty-five-minute time slot to play at Green Mountain Country Fest this year. Thirty minutes would've never been enough. We have too many good songs to choose from." I sat beside my best friend and squeezed his hand. "One more thing I want to run by you." Carter angled his upper body until he faced me. "I want to change our band's name."

His eyes flared. His lips pursed.

"Wait. Listen to me. We need something that sounds

serious. And grown-up. No more Ellis and Hills Band. We're not little kids anymore."

I stood and grabbed a box I'd hid behind the ugly brown couch in Carter's garage.

"What is it?"

"It's a surprise. You've poured your heart and soul into writing new music all summer, and I've barely seen you. It's my way to thank you."

Something passed in the depths of my best friend's eyes. He blinked and chased it away.

"Here," I said as I threw him a black T-shirt.

Carter unfolded it, his eyes never leaving mine. "Carter Hills Band," he said with a tipped eyebrow.

"Yeah, that's our new band name. It's perfect."

"I loved Ellis and Hills Band. Are you sure?"

I nodded, knowing he'd say that. "You are the essence of Ellis and Hills, so it's right we switch to Carter Hills Band. We wouldn't be a band if it weren't for you." I fished a few items from the box. "I got T-shirts, caps, and hoodies. All kinds of merch with our new band name and logo. There you go," I said, handing him the samples.

"Dah, it's too much. It must have cost you a fortune."

I grinned. "No. Daddy got me a deal from a friend of his, and Maurice pitched in as our new sponsor. He loved the idea. He says our logo will look nice in the window display of the restaurant."

Carter stared at me with a slack jaw. I slapped him square in the chest. "Shut your mouth, Cart. You'll catch flies." I winked, and he unfroze.

"It's big, Dah. You sure about this?"

"Oh yes. Never been so sure in my life."

———

Later, in my room, I was painting my nails a sparkling shade of pink when Addison stopped by, her long sleek ponytail bouncing down her back.

We hadn't seen each other in months.

"Hey, girl," she said as she perched herself on the edge of my bed, "how was your summer?" It was the last vacation day before being sophomores.

"I didn't know you were coming over. When did you get back?" I put the nail polish away.

My girlfriend dug her phone from her back pocket to look at the time. "About an hour ago."

I rose to my knees, my attention fully on her.

"I can't believe you're here. How was Paris? I wanna know everything." Addi spent the summer in France in some sort of exchange program to learn French.

"*C'était merveilleux. J'ai eu beaucoup de plaisir, mademoiselle.*" She giggled, and I joined in.

"I can tell your French is good because I have no idea what you just said."

"It was nice. I had a lot of fun, miss. I'll teach you some words. French is the language of love, so you'll impress Jeff. How are you holding up since he's gone?"

I wrinkled my face.

"It's been only seventy-one hours, and I already miss him like crazy. I've been counting the hours since he left. Sorry, I'm being ridiculous. It's super lame."

Addison wolf-whistled. "You're doing the long-distance thing then?"

"Yes. He kept his job at the garage—for now—so he'll come home every few days. Who would have thought Nashville would seem so far?" I sighed. "What about Chris? Did you two make up? Is he still mad you left for the summer after he begged you not to?"

"I haven't told him I'm back yet. I think it's better if I

just face him. You know, this way he won't hang up on me. Or ghost me."

I threw a pillow at my friend.

"You're impossible. Always going for the drama."

"Phoenix says it's my most valuable quality," she said with a shrug. "Anyway, I need to go unpack. I just came over to say hi. I'll see you tomorrow at school." Addi pulled me into a hug. "I've missed you."

"Me too. Glad you're back."

Addison left, and I slumped on my bed. I grabbed my phone from the nightstand and toyed with it. *Come on, Dah, just call him already.*

Jeff answered after the first ring, the sound of his voice enough to soothe me. "Hey you. I was about to call you. How was your day? Missing me already?"

"Like crazy. Rehearsed all afternoon and showed Carter our new merch."

"How did it go?"

I moved my jaw back and forth. "Better than expected. You should've seen his face at first. Anyway, I'm sure it'll grow on him. It was the best decision for the band."

"I'm proud of you, Princess." A huge smile spread across my face. My heartbeat always picked up whenever he called me "Princess."

"Are you all set up?"

"Yeah. I'm sorry I didn't ask you to come along. My parents were making a big deal out of it, and I didn't want them to come—"

"I know, it's okay. Anyway, I might have never left had I tagged along."

"I could've hidden you in the closet. It's small but cozy. I should've thought about it." Just from his tone, I could tell my boyfriend was smiling. "Thanks for the shirt. I keep it under my pillow and bury my face in it each time I think of you. Hey, listen, I need to go. There's like a dorm activity tonight, and someone is knocking on my door. I love you. And I'll call you tomorrow."

"I love you. Have fun."

With my body splayed on the bed and my hands cupping my chest, I fell asleep, wishing my summer vacation could've lasted longer. Much longer.

A knock on my window woke me up. I blinked a few times, trying to reboot my sleepy brain.

Knock. Knock.

My pulse sprinted. Only one person could climb into my room in the middle of the night. I pushed open the curtains to welcome Carter.

"What time is it?" I asked, fighting a yawn as he crawled in.

He raked his fingers through his tousled hair. My lips curled at the sight. "Around midnight. I couldn't sleep. Can I stay here?"

It'd been months since he came over in the middle of the night. The last time was before prom. Before Jeff and I got together.

"Sure. You're always welcome here." Carter offered me a small smile, but his eyes told me he was hurting.

"You wanna talk about it?"

"No. Just need my best friend right now."

Dressed in black sweatpants and a heather gray T-shirt, Carter slid under the covers on the left side of the bed. His hand found mine, and we intertwined our fingers. His head pressed against mine. My heart flipped in my chest as I fell asleep listening to his breathing.

———

I looked at the time on my phone for the tenth time in as many minutes. Where was he? He promised he'd be here. Did he have an accident? Did he forget? No. Impossible. We talked last night, and he told me he had already packed his stuff. I paced the parking lot, my fists on my hips, scanning my surroundings, in case he was here, and I just missed him pulling in. The sun was high and warm for mid-October. The leaves had started turning all shades of orange—Mama always said my hair reminded her of the fall foliage—but the morning air wasn't too crisp yet. Carter and I arrived early because we wanted to immerse ourselves in the vibe of the festival. My parents drove us and left, wanting to spend the day in Green Mountain before coming back to watch us play later. It was one of Carter's rituals before every show. He loved to imprint the crowd's energy on himself. It rubbed off on me, and now I loved doing it too.

A powder-blue van parked next to me, and the back door slid open to reveal four people exiting from it. In rumpled, bed hair, and red-rimmed eyes, they looked like they hadn't had a good night's sleep in a while. Or even a shower. One guy with longish, disheveled blond hair smiled at me, a twinkle in his piercing-blue eyes. I ignored him, balancing on the balls of my feet and hiding my balled hands in my jacket pockets.

"Hey," he said as he halted before me.

I offered him a tight-lipped smile, not willing to start a conversation with a stranger.

He inched closer. I sucked in a breath. Why wouldn't he leave me alone? He studied me for a few seconds, his shoulders slouched forward, a guitar case in one hand. He needed a haircut. And a change of clothes. I looked away, hating how he stared at me.

"Are you here by yourself? Do you need help with something?"

I blew out a breath and rolled my eyes. I forced a curl on my lips and straightened my back. "No. I'm fine," I said in a sharp tone.

"You sure?"

"Yeah. I'm waiting for someone. My boyfriend actually."

It didn't seem to faze him.

"You're playing here today?"

Why didn't he get the message I wanted nothing to do with him?

"Yep. Later tonight."

"Tonight? Wow, you must be good if you scored a night performance." I shrugged, averting my gaze.

A girl with dark skin and brown hair tied in cornrows called after him.

The guy offered me a lopsided grin. "Guess I need to go. Maybe we'll see each other over there," he said, pointing to one of the stages with his thumb.

"Who knows."

"I'll go now. Bye," he said with a wave. He hung a pass matching mine around his neck and followed his friends toward the musicians' entrance.

Weird.

I brought my attention back to the parking lot. In the last five minutes, it had filled up. Now, would I be able to spot Jeff's truck amongst all the others? I doubted it. Pickup trucks all looked the same to me. I sighed. Carter would wonder where I was.

Two men, one with a cowboy hat and a black mustache and the other with a black leather jacket and chaps, parked their motorcycles a few feet from me. I cringed at the sound of their engines.

The younger one wolf-whistled as he gave me a slow and painful once-over. Pig. I folded my arms over my chest, ignoring their snarky comments as they walked past me. Shivers ran through me. Once they were out of sight, I watched a young couple holding hands. They must have been about my age. Sixteen or so. They looked to be in love and shared stupid grins, drinking each other in. I couldn't wait for my own boyfriend to arrive.

One more glance at the time. Jeff was over twenty minutes late. Maybe I should call him. Would I sound desperate? I refused to become a clingy girlfriend. My insides clenched. I hadn't seen Jeff in over a month. Would he—

"Princess—" I pivoted on my heels as soon as I heard my name, forgetting my train of silly thoughts. I could recognize his voice amongst a thousand others. My breath quivered, and I almost tripped on my own feet in my hurry to meet him. I ran into his arms, my heart about to explode. "I've missed you." Jeff spun me around, his lips crashing on mine.

"I thought you wouldn't make it."

Jeff's squeeze tightened around me.

"I'd never miss a show, Dah. You're the most important person in my life."

"What about me?" Carter asked, a sly grin lighting up his face, as he walked toward us.

Jeff put me back on the ground and grabbed Carter in their usual hug. "You too, bro. You look great. And by the way, the new demo you sent me is killer. I can't wait to hear it live."

"Are you home for the entire weekend?" Carter asked.

"Yes."

Sara inched closer and circled Carter's midsection with her arms. Jeff quirked his eyebrows.

"Sara, this is Jeff—"

"OMG, Carter's older brother," she said, in some sort of squawk. She jumped on the ball of her feet, her long raven hair bouncing on her shoulders, and tugged at Jeff's arm, looking at him with her big, round hazelnut irises. "I've heard so much about you." Jeff plastered an *are-you-fucking-joking-right-now* mixed with a *who-the-hell-is-this* smile on his face, gawking at the girl attached to his arm.

"C'mon, Carty, show me around before you do your big show." Sara let go of Jeff, winked at me, and pulled a brooding Carter away.

"Yeah. Go ahead, *Carty*," Jeff shouted after him. A smirk brightened his face when Carter flipped him the finger.

Jeff chuckled, and I joined in.

He turned his head and glanced at me, his eyes drilling holes through my skull.

"Who the fuck is that?"

I circled my arms around him and sighed. "Carter's flavor of the week." My boyfriend clutched my upper arms and leaned back until our eyes met. He frowned. "Don't panic. It's been going on for about a month. Carter is in his rebel phase or something. There's always a new girl. Last week it was Tiffany."

"Tiffany? You're kidding, right?"

"No. And before her it was Aubrey."

"Why didn't you tell me?"

"I don't want Cart to meddle in our relationship, so I stay away from his. Anyway, I'm sure it's no big deal. He's acting out. But it's Carter. He'll grow out of it soon enough. No need to worry."

Jeff pulled me against him, and I pressed my face against his muscular chest, breathing him in. Sandalwood. Cinnamon. God, I'd missed him.

"Fine. I hope you're right. I'm glad I'm back in town for the weekend. We should keep an eye on him." Perhaps Carter would listen to his brother. We were still best friends, but I felt like I'd lost my right to say something about his love life's questionable choices. "Ready for your big show tonight?"

"I think. Will you watch from the side of the stage? I kinda need you around."

"I would have even if you hadn't asked me, Princess. I need to be close to you too."

We kissed and all my doubts vanished.

———

The crowd screamed our name as we walked on stage. Carter and I started playing at Green Mountain Country Fest when we were fourteen. Each year, we attracted a bigger crowd, and likewise, they granted us a bigger time frame to perform. And a bigger stage. This year, we were playing on the second biggest stage as the pre-pre-opening show to the big number at nine, a country music group topping the charts. We'd perform from six to six forty-five, which was quite impressive for two high school kids. Carter and I had to be back home by midnight, and Green Mountain was a three-hour drive from White Crest, so we'd miss the main event.

The breeze tickled the tip of my nose. A whiff of Pretzel and corndog filled the air.

"Hey guys. Thanks for coming. We are Carter Hills Band"—we'd been using the name for the last two months —"and we'll perform our new songs for you tonight." My heart plummeted to my toes. The air in my lungs turned to icebergs, as it always did when we were about to rock the stage. Carter twisted his head my way. "Don't look at them,

Dah. Follow my lead, I'll take care of everything," he whispered. My throat worked. I blew out a cleansing breath. I could do this.

My fingers strummed the first chords of "Heart for Rent," the song Carter wrote at the end of the summer—the one Jeff told me about before he left for college. In all the time my best friend spent locked in his room, he got pretty good at songwriting. He mostly wrote ballads about impossible love stories, soulmates drifting apart, wandering lost souls, or fading friendship.

Deep inside me, I wondered if I was the inspiration behind some of the lyrics. After all, I was pretty sure I'd shattered Carter's heart even if I'd never found the courage to ask him about it, fearing what might happen if I opened that door.

Carter's voice, husky and low, attacked the first verse.

> **I saw you first that day**
> **Wearing a red dress**
> **Your hair was flying around**
>   **your face**
> **Sunshine was brushing**
>   **your skin**
> **Lighting up your freckles like a**
>   **road map to paradise**
> **I stood there, frozen, mesmer-**
>   **ized by your smile**
> **I saw you first, girl...**

I joined in on the chorus and caught sight of Jeff watching us from the side of the stage. Every time he glanced at me with that much heat, my insides liquified. No doubt Jeffrey Hills possessed every bit of my heart.

Hot tears welled in my eyes.

Emotions bubbled inside me as I stood on the stage with Carter and Jeff on each side of me. I loved Jeff with everything I had. But my heart was also a mess when I remembered how I hurt my best friend to get there.

I recovered myself just in time to add back-vocals to Carter's performance.

The large crowd cheered us on. Flutters took over my stomach. The hyperactive kind. The sky slowly turned into a canvas of orange, purple, and pink stripes. I filled my lungs with the mountain air. Carter winked as he strummed the opening chords of "Monkey Business," a more upbeat song with a catchy chorus. I joined him and failed at hiding my smile when I sang the verses. The silly lyrics chased my emotional overload away.

> **...I thought there was a hippo**
> **in your closet**
> **A monkey hidden under**
> **your bed**
> **I thought I saw a lion in your**
> **kitchen**
> **And a snake hanging from the**
> **chandelier**
> **Because that's what your love**
> **does to me, baby**
> **You turn my world**
> **upside down**
> **My imagination runs wild**
> **I can become a pirate, a ghost**
> **hunter, or even an**
> **astronaut**
> **There's nothing I can't do**
> **No, nothing I can't do**
> **As long as you're beside me...**

The show ended, and both Carter and I now had permanent smiles branded on our faces.

"We were awesome, Dah. Listen to the crowd. We've killed it." Carter draped his arm around my shoulders and hugged me. "We're the real deal. One day, we'll be the ones headlining this festival. You and me."

Playing live music always made me jittery. However, the rush compared to nothing else. As if the world wasn't big enough to contain both of us. As if we could go on for days without sleeping or eating. My eyes met my boyfriend's, and I realized he had the same effect on me.

"We nailed it, Cart. Do you really think we'll make it big one day?" My best friend leaned closer, and his warm breath tickled my earlobe.

"I do, Dah. Trust me, we will."

Jeff kissed me when we joined him backstage and grabbed the guitar case from my hand as we followed him to his truck.

"Where's Sara?" I asked Carter as we stacked our stuff in the back.

He shrugged. "Gone. Her girlfriends are here, and she must be with them. Anyway, we broke up." Carter focused his attention on something else. The conversation was over. "Are you driving back with your parents?"

"No. They agreed to let me ride with you guys. They must be on their way home already. I'm sorry your parents couldn't make it."

Except for Jeff, who never missed any of our shows, Carter's parents rarely followed us around. They came to every in-town performance but never to our shows outside White Crest.

"It's fine. Let's not talk about this and just enjoy the festival before we need to get going."

The three of us joined the singing crowd before the

main stage, and eating hot dogs from one of the food stands, we watched some of our idols as they took the stage. I was singing at the top of my lungs when Jeff screamed my way so I could hear him over the music.

"We need to get going, Princess. I don't want to piss off your parents, or they won't trust me anymore." I sighed. "I'm sorry." Jeff walked me to his truck and placed his keys in my hand. "I'll go get Carter. Lock the doors after you." He kissed me, his tongue and lips hungry for me. "I'll be right back."

Warmth radiated through me. My entire body vibrated with happiness.

Jeff disappeared behind the row of trucks parked on the left side of the festival's entrance as I hauled myself on the backseat. In the distance, I heard people screaming. I looked at the time. The main event was about to take the stage—no doubt Carter would have a hard time leaving. He'd been dying to watch those guys perform live for years. In the last few weeks, we'd tried to talk our parents into letting us rent a hotel room for the night, so we could attend the entire festival, but they all refused. I slouched in the seat. The adrenaline from our show had faded, and my eyelids weighed heavy now.

The guys climbed in the truck, and soon enough, the scenery changed from luscious green mountains—yeah, intuitive—to lakes and plains. I loved Green Mountain. It was so quiet. And the air smelled better. Cleaner. One day, I'd get a house there. A log cabin. Or a farmhouse. And a big piece of land. Not that I didn't like White Crest. It had the small-town charm and was closed to Nashville, but Green Mountain was *it* for me. Every time I went there, a sense of peace filled every inch of me. I felt at home. As if the world had no end.

I wasn't sure when I fell asleep. Carter and Jeff were

arguing about some football thing I had no interest in, and I must've dozed off.

"Hey Princess," Jeff whispered, his face a hair's breadth from mine, bringing me out of my slumber.

"Hey," I said, my voice croaky and rough after our night. Only lit up by the streetlights, Jeff looked mesmerizing, his features darker than in bright sunlight, his eyes beaming as he looked at me.

"People are going to the creek tomorrow, and there's a barbecue later. I know it is Sunday, but Carter and I are going. You think your mama will let you? We'll be home before curfew. I kind of want to spend time with you. Far from our parents' watch."

I stretched my arms over my head and looked around. "Where's Cart?"

"Home. I've been watching you sleep for the last fifteen minutes. He said I was a creep."

"You kind of are. But I love you no matter what."

I looped my arms around my boyfriend's neck and pulled him toward me. Our lips moved together, and I injected heat in our kiss, unable to resist him.

"Dah, don't kiss me like this when your dad can walk in on us anytime. I'll be a dead man." I pushed him in the chest.

"Let me talk to Mama about tomorrow. I wanna go. We'd be able to kiss all we want. Wait. Don't you have to drive back to Nashville after dinner?"

"Nah, don't have classes on Monday morning. Change of schedule. It's okay."

Jeff lifted me up from the backseat and lowered me to the ground. He kissed me one last time. His lips tasted like hot chocolate and sour candy. My heart flipped around in my chest. I whispered against his mouth, "I don't want to let you go." I fastened my grip around his neck. "I wish this night would never end."

Jeff pressed his hard-on against my tummy. Heat flowed through me. A little smile grazed my lips, and I cupped him over his washed-out denims.

"Princess—Your dad—How can I—Jesus."

His erection twitched in my hand. My boyfriend lowered his hands from my burning cheeks to my chest. I melted against him.

"Tomorrow night. You and me," he said, pulling my bottom lip between his teeth. Desire shot through me. It pooled between my thighs. I ground my hips against Jeff's hard cock. He kneaded my breasts, toying with my hard nipples. A moan tumbled out of my mouth. "Oh yes, baby. I know exactly what you need."

Heat rushed to my face. I was grateful for the darkness, not willing to let Jeff see how much his words affected me. *Tomorrow night*, I reminded myself. I swallowed hard.

"I'd like that. A lot."

Jeff kissed me, stealing every ounce of oxygen from my lungs. On wobbly legs, I ambled toward my house, my heart tap-dancing in my chest, my body humming, and happiness waltzing inside my bloodstream.

"Good night, Princess."

"Night."

———

"I'll go find Phen and see you guys later," Carter said, jumping off Jeff's truck. "I'm not sure I wanna witness you two being all in love." Our glance landed on each other, and our eyes did the talking, exposing every ache stashed in our hearts.

It doesn't have to be that way, mine said. *I hate when we're weird around each other.*

I'll be fine, Carter's replied. *One day. Gimme more time.*

Don't lose faith in us. I love you.

I know…Dah. I love you too.

I'm sorry. Please don't push me out. Don't push us out.

His didn't say anything further.

Carter bowed his head, waving at me—at us—as he strolled away.

Jeff moved to the backseat next to me and circled my wrist as I leaned back and shut my eyes, tears ready to flow out. "Princess, what just happened?"

I shrugged and sniffled. "I'm trying to make things right with your bother."

"Is it working?"

"I don't know." I sighed and blinked to keep my tears at bay. "Can we just enjoy each other for tonight? I'll deal with him tomorrow. You'll be gone by the morning, and I really want you to keep up the promise you made last night," I said, the corner of my lips curving into a small smile.

"You do?" Jeff's eyes lit up, and it soothed everything inside me. My happiness returned.

"That's all I've been dreaming about last night, and the only thing that's been on my mind all day."

"Then scoot over, we need to make ourselves comfortable."

Jeff's mouth claimed mine as I shifted on the seat. His fingers entangled in my hair, and one hand curled around my waist, anchoring me.

A yelp escaped my lips when his tongue dived further into my mouth.

"You sure you're ready for me to touch you?"

I nodded.

My heart banged against my ribs.

I panted as if I'd just run a marathon.

Jitters bounced around in my body, igniting my inner thighs.

Jeff tightened his grip around my waist, and I melted in his embrace.

"Please," I begged, thoughts racing in my head, wondering what he'd do to me. I gasped as he cupped one breast, now eager to feel his hands under my clothes.

Jeff kissed my throat and collarbones. His head traveled lower, his tongue teasing the strip of my skin peeking out between the hem of my shirt and the top of my jeans. My body stiffened, then relaxed as his tongue drew circles on my flesh.

I knitted my fingers in his hair, not sure what I should do with my own hands.

My boyfriend pushed my shirt up, exposing my midsection.

His eyes sparkled as he raised them to watch me.

"Do you wanna stop?"

I shook my head, biting on my lower lip, silencing the cries threatening to come out of my mouth. My cheeks felt a thousand degrees warmer. Jeff's fingers traced a line along the seam of my pants between my legs, and my vision blurred. Sensations I never knew existed filled me.

"More," I whispered.

His mouth crashed on mine, feasting on my lips, as he unbuttoned my pants. He slid one finger underneath the waistband of my underwear, and my hips buckled off the seat as he rubbed the spot aching for him.

With both hands, I clutched his shoulders, digging my nails in his flesh through his shirt.

Heat billowed inside me.

Would I fall apart or get revived?

Shivers moved up my back.

Jeff's touch set my body on fire.

"You like that?" he asked as he entered one finger inside me—gently—studying my face at the same time. "You want to keep going?"

I nodded; my words locked inside me.

My body buzzed with ache and need. My hips swayed, chasing pleasure.

My eyes closed, my lids now too heavy, and my lips parted.

Was that what an out-of-the-body experience felt like?

None of my cells belonged to me anymore, Jeff's magnetism too strong, each inch of me craving him.

Lightning ran through me as I fell apart.

I could feel Jeff smiling against my lips as I fought to keep my eyes open.

"How did you do this?" I asked, my voice croaky, once I landed back on Earth. "I can't believe we never did this before."

"You liked it?" I bobbed my head, still rushing to get my words out. "I love you, Princess. And I love making you feel good." His lips tasted my trembling ones.

Fire burned inside me.

Jeff turned me into a molten pile of lusting flesh.

"Ready to join our friends now?"

I shook my head. "No. I want to make you see stars too."

"You don't have to," he said, sitting back on his ankles between my legs.

My voice shuddered. "Let me." I begged him with my eyes. "You need this as much as I do." I could see the contour of his erection pushing against the zipper of his jeans.

Jeff's breathing sped up. I rubbed him over his pants

before he could argue and squeezed him. His eyes fluttered close.

I moved forward and pushed him down, straddling him as I freed his dick and curled my hand around him. A series of groans left his mouth.

I pumped his warm silky skin, enjoying each growl escaping his lips.

It didn't take long before Jeff's thick cum covered my hand—and his stomach.

We stood there, breathing each other's air, lost in our own bubble, unable to break apart.

"I'll never be able to drive away tomorrow morning. You owe me, Princess. I always miss you so damn much."

A wide smile stretched my lips, mirroring his.

His words played with all my heartstrings. I inhaled to keep my emotions bottled in.

Jeff's thumb grazed the skin of my cheek. "Don't be sad. Let's enjoy tonight."

"Yes. I'm sure Addi must be wondering where we are."

We cleaned ourselves up and stumbled out of the truck, drunk on love and all the things we just did.

———

Six months later

I twirled around, looking at my reflection in the mirror. "You look perfect, Dah. Stop worrying so much."

Addison sat on my bed, reading a magazine as I changed for the sixth time.

"I look like a sixteen-year-old."

"Duh, because you are, dummy."

"I know." I threw a pillow at her. "But what if he sees me as a kid? We haven't seen each other in two months. It's enough time for a guy to find another girl. One older, wiser, and who's ready to put out. Why would he wait for me?"

Addison sat straighter. "The guy's madly in love with you, Dah. He'll wait for you a thousand years if you'd ask him."

I tied my hair in a high ponytail. I cringed and let my hair fall back over my shoulders.

"I guess you're right, but it still seems like a dream most of the time. Even more when I don't see him for weeks. Since he got that new job in Nashville last fall, he hasn't come home as often."

"Stop whining. You'll have your man all to yourself the entire summer. Don't overthink everything." She put the magazine down. "When will he be here?"

I glanced at the time. "In two hours. I'll never be ready in time."

"Chill, Dah. What am I here for?"

Jeff pulled into my driveway twelve minutes after Addison left. We had plans to meet with her later. There was a Spring Fling party tonight at the fair, and all our friends were going.

I rushed to him before he had time to kill the engine.

I yanked his door open, almost ripping the hinges off, and straddled him, my back pressing against the steering wheel as I kissed him senseless.

"I can't believe you're home," I said against his lips. Jeff clamped my waist and pulled me closer. I could feel every inch of him twitching underneath me. I peppered kisses all over his face.

"Woman, you feel good. And you taste even better." His fingertips grazed my nape, the back of my arms, the length of my throat, sending shivers through my core.

Heat filled me.

My pulse doubled its rhythm.

My toes curled.

Jeff fisted my hair and pressed his forehead to mine, his breathing heavy.

"I'll never get enough of you, Princess. I can't believe we've been apart for months." His large hands cradled my face. "I love you, Dahlia. I fucking love you."

Fireworks burst inside me. "I love you, Jeff."

"You're coming home with me for dinner?" he asked. I bobbed my head. "Then I need to tell you something first." My breath quickened, and I pressed my hands over his muscular chest. Jeff scratched the side of his face, now avoiding my eyes.

"Hey, talk to me," I said, a jittery feeling in my tummy. I cradled his cheeks. A shadow passed through his eyes. In a low voice, I continued, "You're scaring me. What is it?"

"I've been lying to you. Since October— I—How am I supposed to tell you? Damn it." His palm hit the middle console between the front seats.

With both hands, I pushed him against his seat.

"Hey, just tell me. Stop messing around. It's not funny." Anger sliced my voice. Waves of angst danced in my stomach. The cabin of the truck closed around us. The air became rare and thick. "What is it?"

"I dropped out of college—"

I tried to talk, but nothing came out of my throat. I went blank. His words appeared to reach me after a few seconds, traveling through the fog in my mind. I couldn't breathe as if I were free-falling from a sky-high building

"—Last fall."

My hands pressed against my banging heart. I inhaled, trying to stay calm. I swallowed a few times, then cleared my throat.

"Care to explain?"

"I was unhappy, Princess. Like it took all I had to go to class every morning. I tried. I did." Jeff's hands framed my face, and his lips brushed mine. "I'm sorry I lied to you. I couldn't say anything. You know my parents—"

An infinite number of knots strangled my stomach. This wasn't good.

After a long minute, I found my voice. "Tell me this is a joke. That you're messing with me." Jeff shook his head, his gaze down. "I can't believe you did that. And that you didn't tell me. I don't know which one is upsetting me the most." I punched his chest, my eyes filling with hot tears. "You're messing with your future."

"Business is not my thing. Spending hours in a classroom, listening to a boring teacher lecturing me about stuff I don't care about isn't either." Jeff huffed a laugh. "I've been thriving. Everything is good. You don't even know if you want to go to college yourself, so you should understand where I come from."

"It's not the point. I still have time to choose a path." I gritted my teeth. "You can't be a college drop-out at nineteen. You need a plan. This is not right." I closed my eyes and slowed my breathing.

Mama would flip a switch when she learned about it. Jeff's mama too.

My boyfriend sucked in a breath. It looked painful. He knitted his fingers through mine and met my eyes. "Don't cry, Princess. I'm happy. Don't worry about me. I've worked over fifty hours a week for months."

"You've got a steady job?"

"I've been working at this pub in Nashville. With the tips, I've made some great money, and I've met all kinds of people from the music industry. I have contacts, Dah. Lots of them. For you and Carter. There's this guy I want you two to meet. He'll come to see you play. Anyway, I've been saving money to buy a house. I couch-surfed and piled out each dollar. All of it. And I saved the money I made working at the garage too. We'll be fine. I'll take care of you. I want a place for us. When you turn eighteen, I want you to come live with me. I want us."

I blinked.

"You what? Whoa. There's a lot to take in here. You lived on other people's couches for months and didn't tell me. Was it even safe? This is worse than I first thought." Could Jeff read the hurt in my eyes? The lining of my throat itched. "You didn't trust me with your secret—" My voice cracked. Jeff's hands searched mine, but I pushed him back. "No. It's not fine with me. You should've told me. Does Carter know?" He shook his head. "We care about you." Tears rolled down my cheeks, and I stifled the sob forming deep inside me. "It's not fair." I palmed his chest. I didn't recognize the boy before me. "Were you ever going to tell any of us, or did you intend to keep it a secret forever?"

My cheeks burned.

My lips tingled.

My heart heaved in my throat.

"What else did you lie about?"

"Nothing. I swear."

"And I should believe you? Forget it. I'm done. I won't stay here and watch you throw your future away."

I opened the door and jumped from the truck, storming toward my house.

Jeff's footsteps resonated on the cobblestones as he rushed to catch me.

"Princess, let's talk about it. Don't overreact. It'll all be fine. I promise. I'm doing this for us."

"Don't 'Princess' me. You have no right. Don't tell me you dropped out of college for me. I might be young and inexperienced, but I'm not stupid." I stopped in my tracks, out of breath.

"Dahlia—" Jeff leaned in to kiss me. I stepped back.

"No. Don't." The words scorched my tongue. Hurt flashed in his eyes. I stretched my arm to keep him a foot away from me. My heart pounded. And broke for the man I thought I knew everything about. Fury boiled inside me. "Do you plan to work in that pub for the rest of your life?" My fingernails ripped the flesh of my palms. I pivoted on my heels to keep my back to my boyfriend, refusing to let him see my face, and folded my arms over my chest.

"Why are you so upset? I have everything figured out. Wait until you meet that guy. I'm doing it for the band. For you and Carter. And for us. It'll all work out in the end. Don't you trust me?"

Jeff clamped his fingers on my upper arms and forced me to turn around until our faces were level. Some of my anger vanished. Jeff had this ability to calm me down, even when I was mad at him. Something in the way he stared at me soothed the storm in my belly.

"Yes. I do. I know you'd never do anything to hurt me. Or your brother. I'm upset, though. Upset that you didn't trust me. I always trust you so I can't understand why you weren't honest with me."

Pain filled Jeff's dark irises. "I trust you. But I was scared you'd be disappointed in me. And the last thing I want is for you to be upset with me. I love you. As if my heart doesn't know how to beat when you're not around. I—"

I silenced him with a kiss. "I feel the same, but it doesn't excuse what you did."

We kissed until we both needed a fresh intake of air. Until our hearts beat in synch again.

"What can I do to earn your forgiveness?" A sly grin appeared on his face.

Tingles filled every inch of me.

I huffed and rolled my shoulders back. I raised one finger. "First, don't ever lie to me again. I might be just a kid, but I'm strong enough to hear all you have to say. If you want us to work out, you have to tell me when you're sad. Or unhappy."

"Won't happen again. And you're not a kid, Dahlia Ellis. You're a strong, smart, and resourceful girl. You're my woman. And I'll never let you go. I'll make you proud."

My body overflew with heat.

How could Jeff be so sure we'd last forever?

I raised a second finger. "And you need to come clean. Your family loves you. And I'm in love with you. For better or for worse." Another layer of anger left me. "No more secrets."

My hand found Jeff's, and we made it back to the truck.

"Are we okay?" he asked, lingering pieces of fear swimming in his eyes.

I nodded. "We will be. Actually, there's one more thing." Jeff halted and studied me, his head hanging low.

"Name it."

I rose to my tiptoes and whispered in his ear, "You know that thing you do with your fingers?" I clenched my thighs together and bit my lower lip. "I'd like you to do it to me later tonight."

My body sizzled, all excited at the mere thought of it.

Jeff's hand molded around the back of my neck, and he kissed me. I opened my mouth and welcomed his tongue inside, yearning for him to touch me. Everywhere.

"I can't wait for dinner to be over," he said, breathless.

"Me too. Let's get you home first. You'll need me when

you break the news to your parents. And please tell Carter beforehand. I know he'd hate to be the last one to know. You owe him that."

Jeff dropped his head and shoulders and followed me, never letting go of my hand.

7

JEFFREY

With both hands, I pressed my brother's shoulders until he sat on my bed. Carter's eyes traveled between Dahlia's and mine.

"Okay. You two are scaring me. What's the look on your faces about? Did someone die?" I shook my head. "Did you get Dahlia pregnant? Oh shit. Disturbing. I don't even want to know if you two are— Oh god, I don't need those images in my head. Okay, I'll ask it. Dah, are you pregnant?"

We both screamed "NO" at the same time.

Carter blew out a long breath and ran both hands over his face. "What is it then? Tell me. I hate this game."

I sat on a chair facing him, and Dahlia sat beside him on the bed.

I told Carter everything. Even the part where I wanted to buy a house for Dahlia and me. His eyes clouded for a split second.

"Are you fucking with me?" Carter sprung to his feet. "Mom will kill you. Or maybe not, since you're her favorite."

I gave Carter a pointed look. No. We wouldn't go there. Not tonight. I knew how he felt about our mom being more invested in my life than his. We'd talked about it a lot over the years. But our dad was a die-hard fan of Carter's music, so in my mind, it kind of balanced out.

My brother studied me for a moment.

"Are you gonna get a job? Or are you still thinking about enlisting? It's a bad idea, but if you do, you know Mom wants you to wait until you're twenty-one, right?"

"I'm not. I'm not sure it's what I'm supposed to do. We'll see. I'm meeting with Brendan's dad tomorrow. He's hiring for the new strip mall they're building by the sports center. He might have a job for me. In construction."

Carter worked his jaw.

"Fine. What's your plan for tonight? I know you have one. You always do."

"I'll tell Mom and Dad everything, and the three of us will drive somewhere afterward because I don't want to spend my night listening to them telling me I'm screwing up my life."

"Let's do this." Carter rose and clapped my shoulder. "I'm in your corner, big bro."

Seated beside each other at the kitchen table, Dahlia and I squeezed hands under the table. For the last twenty minutes, we'd been exchanging gazes with Carter. I hoped Dahlia and he understood I didn't tell them right away about dropping out of college to protect them in case my parents asked questions. Or was I too much of a coward and feared what they'd think of me? It didn't matter anymore. They both heard me out and chose to back me up.

I glanced at the plate in front of me, still half-full. I couldn't eat, my stomach too tight.

Dahlia's thumb drew circles over my knuckles. I breathed in and delivered the news.

Mom choked on a green bean. Dad harrumphed but said nothing.

Without a word, Mom rose from her chair and disappeared into the kitchen. We heard her blowing her nose. Was she crying? My dad's eyes burrowed into mine. "I knew this day would come. I told your mama she can't force you to follow a path that isn't yours. Give her some time. She'll come around. But don't expect to live here rent-free, son. You want to act like a man, then I'll treat you like one."

"Yes sir," I said, lowering my gaze. I chugged my glass of water and cleared my throat. "There's something else." My dad's eyes rounded. "I'm buying a house. For Dahlia and me."

"Jeff—"

"Let me finish. I know she'll be eighteen in a little over a year. I'll wait. There's no rush. But when she's ready, she's agreed to move in with me. And I've saved enough money to put a down payment on a small house in the neighborhood. In this economy, it's better to buy than to rent an apartment." I gulped my girl's glass of water in one sip—now that mine was empty—trying to erase the trail of fire down my throat.

"I agree that real estate is a great investment. And knowing you, I'm sure you've taken every cent into account. But I still don't understand why you're in a rush to settle down."

"Dad—"

My father pressed both hands against the wooden table. The room fell silent. "We'll talk about it later. Right now, you guys should head out. Have some fun. Let me deal with your mama." He fished a couple of twenties from his pockets and handed it to Carter. "Go grab a burger somewhere. Just don't miss curfew, okay?"

The three of us nodded and hurried to my truck.

I blew out a long breath, filled with angst and fear—and relief—as I got behind the wheel.

"Spring Fling?" Carter asked from the backseat.

"Hell yes," Dahlia and I said at the same time. I clamped her hand and kissed the back of it.

"Then let's go before Dad changes his mind and runs after us," Carter said. I turned on the ignition and drove away from our parents' house with my two partners in crime.

Spring Fling was just as I remembered. Fifteen to twenty-something-year-olds taking over the fairgrounds with live music and the punch probably already spiked by now. Addison and Phoenix, Dahlia and Carter's friends, met us as soon as we parked the truck. Phoenix led Carter away, and Addison stuck with us. Brendan and a few guys from high school were on their way too.

I locked my arm around Dah's waist and pulled her close to me. I'd missed her too much in the last few months to let her wander away from me, even if it was only for a few hours.

The night passed in a blur.

I dropped Carter home at eleven, wanting to spend a little time alone with my girl. We drove to an empty field a mile from our street. I hadn't even killed the engine before Dahlia was on my lap, her tongue down my throat.

My fingers entangled in her hair.

Her hands slipped under my shirt and traced the ridges of my chest muscles. I shivered.

My mouth claimed hers, desperate to taste her lips.

Dahlia's floral scent enveloped me. Every fiber of my body reacted to her closeness.

My hand traveled to her thigh, caressing the soft flesh under the hem of her dress. She tilted her head back, and I feasted on her neck.

"Touch me already," she begged me. Her breathing hitched—and so did mine—as everything around us faded away.

Forty minutes later, I drove Dahlia back home. She wouldn't let go of me, her cheeks flushed and her lips red and swollen.

"I'll see you in the morning, Princess." I dried a lone tear sliding down her face. "I'm not going away anymore. In one year, we'll be living together. Hold on, okay?"

She nodded. And I kissed away all her pain.

———

Two weeks later, we were in Redfield, Kentucky. Carter Hills Band was playing at some musical fest. It wasn't a big thing, but exposure was exposure. And I loved going on the road with Carter and Dahlia. Our parents trusted us to go by ourselves now that I was almost twenty.

Four days ago, I shot a message to that country music executive I met in Nashville. He and I talked a couple of times while I worked at the pub, and after I played some of Carter and Dahlia's songs to him, he convinced a friend of his, a manager on the rise, to come to see them play. So here we were, early in the morning, the band getting ready to impress that Riley-guy.

My brother and girlfriend were jamming, trying new arrangements behind a big white tent when a guy with tousled blond hair and wrinkled, stained clothes walked up to us.

He came a few feet from Dahlia. She raised her eyes and studied him for a minute, a frown etching her forehead. "Are you the girl from Green Mountain Country Fest?" he asked. "The one in the parking lot who gave me stinky eyes?"

Dahlia's lips pursed.

"It's you. I swear it's you. I was in a blue van—"

"I remember." My girl brought her attention back to the guitar in her hands, ignoring him.

"Listen. I've been watching you play for quite some time. Oh, sorry. I'm Stud, by the way."

Carter acknowledged him with a small nod.

"Anyway, I've been following you guys for a while. And I want to join your band."

Carter burst out laughing. "You're joking, right?"

Stud shook his head. "No. I think I can help you bring your music to another level. I've been a roadie forever. And I'm a huge fan, in case you wonder. You guys are the next big thing. I can tell. But you need my help. I'm the bandmate you never knew you needed. Just try me out."

Carter shook his head. "Not today, buddy. Sorry. We have some guy coming to see us play later."

"Gimme an hour. If I don't convince you by ten o'clock, then I'll never bother you ever again. Please, just give me a shot."

Carter and Dahlia exchanged a gaze. They never needed words to understand each other. It'd always been that way for as long as I could remember. They could read each other with ease. Once they came to some sort of mutual agreement, they both stared at me. I shrugged. My opinion didn't matter. It wouldn't change anything. But I loved the idea of giving this guy a chance to prove himself. They had nothing to lose. Stud looked like a dirty hippie, but maybe he was that good. Who knew?

Carter moved to sit beside Dahlia on the second chair facing me.

"Thirty minutes. Top. Show us what you've got."

"You want me to play the guitar, the drums, or the keyboard?"

"Whatever, man. Impress us."

"I'll get my stuff and be right back."

Stud hurried away.

Carter turned to Dahlia. "Are we making a mistake?"

"I don't know," she said. "But he's overconfident, so he must know his stuff. I don't know—"

Carter looked at me. "What do you think, bro?"

"What have you got to lose? I agree with Dah. He's either good or a cocky fool. Let's hope it's the first one." I lowered my voice. "Here he comes."

Stud came back with a keyboard under his arms, a guitar strapped to his back, and a large grin plastered to his face.

He settled and offered us another one of his sly grins. "Are you ready to be amazed?" Yeah, he better be incredible, or Carter would kick his ass. "Pick any song. Don't tell me which one, I'll join in."

Stud delivered. Carter had to snap his mouth shut a few times as Stud played with them. How could one man be that talented? He wasn't a guitar prodigy like Carter but more like a musical genius. Someone who could adapt to any song as if he'd played it thousands of times before. Dahlia's eyes widened as she strummed the last chord. She glanced at me, asking for my silent blessing.

Stud jumped to his feet. "Well, I'll let you think about it. I'll see you later." And as fast as he arrived, he strolled away, blending into the growing crowd.

Carter cleared his throat, his eyes bright and wide. He blinked a few times before speaking. "Okay. That was intense. Am I the only one blown away right now?"

"That was insane. The guy can play. I know my vote

doesn't count, but I'd die to hear him on stage with you later. For two or three songs. See how it sounds."

Dahlia, still mute, finally spoke. "Carter, do you think Stud has the sound we've been looking for now for a while? The one we said we've been missing? That edge? I don't know. He fit right in. I'm afraid to admit it, but he blew my mind."

"Yeah. I think he could be it. That solo he added on "Far Away" was intuitive and on point."

"Jeff, go find him. If he can get a decent change of clothes, we'll try him."

"What about that manager?" I asked.

"We'll play with and without Stud. Let's see what he thinks. Tell Stud he isn't in the band, just filling in."

"I'm on it," I said as I clapped Carter on the shoulder and kissed Dahlia on the forehead, before vanishing into the crowd.

Carter Hills Band rocked onstage. The crowd went crazy as Stud joined them for the last two songs.

My entire body vibrated from the energy-filled air.

I hoped the manager would be as impressed as the screaming fans.

People rushed toward the band to get autographs once they moved away from the stage. Dahlia beamed. Carter's face lit up. And me? I was so proud of them. I wasn't officially in the band, but I loved how they included me as if I belonged.

A man with brown hair, hardly older than me, broke free from the line, nearing my brother.

"You're Carter Hills?" he asked, his voice even, and seriousness written all over his face. He wore a brown dress shirt rolled at the elbows, black pants, and dark shoes.

Carter stuck his hand out. "Yes, sir."

They shook hands. "Don't call me sir, please. I'm not

that old. I'm Riley." The man turned to face Dahlia. "Hi, Dahlia, nice to meet you." His gaze landed on me next. "And you must be Jeff; I've heard a lot about you too."

"It's a pleasure," I said, holding out my hand to shake his. "Thanks for coming today."

"It wasn't a hard choice. After I heard the demo you gave Dan, I knew I had to meet with the band before someone else did."

Pride filled me. I knew it. I resisted the temptation to jump around and hug everyone.

Riley brought his focus back to Carter and Dahlia.

"You guys were great up there. I'd like to hear more about your music and meet up with you. Soon. Very soon. What do you think?"

Carter pinched his lips together and steeled his back. "Let me talk with my bandmate for a second, would you?"

Carter tugged at Dahlia's elbow and led her away.

They talked for at least five minutes before joining us.

"We'd like to meet with you, Mr.—"

"Burns. Riley Burns." He held out his hand to shake all of ours. "That's settled. Oh, and one more thing. Who was that guy playing with you?"

"His name's Stud. We were trying him today, see how he'd sound. For now, it was a one-time thing."

"If I were you, I'd bring him on board full-time. He's crazy talented. Other groups might poach him after hearing him play today. I know I would."

"We'll see what we can do. We can't promise anything yet."

"Carter, Dahlia, you're both talented. And your song-writing is top-notch. But having a guy like Stud in your band is a sure thing that could lead to being signed by a major label or bring you to another level. The three of you together, it's dynamite. Think about it." Riley handed

Dahlia his card. "Call me next week, we'll schedule an appointment."

The moment he was out of sight, Carter lifted me in his arms and spun me around like I weighed close to nothing.

And then, once he put me back on my feet, he spun Dahlia around. Finally, it was my turn to lift Dahlia in my arms. My mouth landed on hers, and with all the passion running through my veins, I kissed her.

Someone whistled, and we brought our attention back to the lined-up fans waiting to get pictures and autographs.

"All y'all better hold on to these pictures because these guys will be famous, and you'll be able to tell everyone you met them here today," I said to them, becoming the photographer of the hour, snapping pictures of my two most favorite people in the world with the crowd handing me their phones.

Hours later, Carter leaned close as he put his guitar case in the cargo bed of my truck. "I owe you one, big bro. You might have changed our lives today." I pulled him into a hug.

"I'd do just about anything for you, brother."

———

I didn't join Dahlia and Carter at their meeting in one of Nashville's high-rise buildings with Riley Burns a month later, but I tagged along. Mr. Ellis drove us there and went inside with them. As a business lawyer, he was their official representative. I'd do anything to be a part of their band if I had any musical talent whatsoever. Music was Carter and Dahlia's thing. Not mine.

I needed to pave my own path. Find a career I'd thrive at. Whatever it meant. I had no idea what it was yet except that being a third wheel to Carter Hills Band was not it.

I spent the three-hours-and-forty-seven minutes the meeting lasted in the pub where I used to work. Nashville had become a second home to me, and I'd miss coming back here next year, but I was set on buying a house, settling down with my girl, and becoming someone she'd be proud of.

Once their meeting was over, Dahlia, her dad, and Carter met up with me at the bar.

I held my breath when they walked in.

"How was it?" I asked, my heart thundering in my chest the moment they took a seat around the table.

"Incredible," Dahlia said, her gaze full of stars.

"I don't know where to start," Carter added, a large smile splitting his face in two.

"Listen, kids. I'll review their offer. But if we can get this Stud—" Mr. Ellis's eyes searched the papers before him on the table "—Burgess to join the band, they'll increase their offer. So far, it sounds good. I'll get a few colleagues to make the required verifications, but this could be big. Bigger than you ever expected. You need to be ready for this. Because if we reach a deal, your lives might never be the same ever again. You need to be sure it's what you want. Fame, tours, and all of this."

Mr. Ellis's words lingered between the four of us. Dahlia grabbed Carter's hand and mine and squeezed them tight.

As Dahlia's dad drove us back home, we settled on the back seat of his SUV, and I circled her shoulder with my arm. Carter sat in the passenger seat, too tall to be comfortable back here. The air in the truck sizzled with electricity. Nobody said a word. Carter looked out through the window, Mr. Ellis played low music through the stereo, and I just enjoyed the peace and calm with my girl nested in my arms.

Dahlia cocked her head to look at me. "Thank you," she said with sparks in her eyes and a warm smile, the one she reserved only for me. The one that could bring me to my knees and make me do anything she'd ask of me.

"For what?"

"Everything. Riley. Being here. Loving me."

My lips found her temple. "Princess, I'd do anything for you. You should know this by now."

She embedded her head in the crook of my neck, and with her body molded to mine, she drifted to sleep.

My heart doubled in size.

I breathed out and closed my eyes. Sharing this moment, right here, right now, with Carter and Dahlia was more important than anything else in my life.

———

Six months later

"This is it. Our first single is playing on the radio," Dahlia announced as she sat between my legs, facing the bonfire. The four of us, including Stud—now officially a member of Carter Hills Band—were enjoying a night by the creek with our friends. A little celebration of our own.

"I'm so proud of you, Princess."

The smile she offered me broke me into pieces and built me back up, my heart warmer, bigger, and shinier.

"Our album is coming out in less than a month, and we already have over fifteen interviews scheduled. This is insane," Carter exclaimed, bringing a bottle of beer to his lips. None of us were of legal drinking age, but since tonight was a celebration, I offered to be the designated driver. My brother had earned the right to have some fun and let go for a night.

Dahlia and he had turned seventeen a few months back.

Five weeks ago, I closed the deal on a two-car garage, white front-porch-swing house. The exterior needed a good paint job since the once-gray paint was all chipped, and the kitchen and bathroom needed to be remodeled, but I didn't care. It was home. I'd work days and nights to make this place beautiful before Dahlia moved in. We chose the house together, and she picked up shades of paint to refresh the kitchen cabinets because my girlfriend had a gift for turning ugly things into gems. In a couple of months, this place would be ours.

Until Dahlia could move in with me, I took Stud in as a roommate. He needed a place to stay, and I had a spare room. And his monthly rent covered half of the mortgage. The guy couldn't live forever in a van. Stud was easygoing and nice and fit right in with us.

For the last six months, I'd been working in construction—Brendan's dad hired me—which was pretty useful with my new house project. I also picked up shifts at the garage I used to work at on the weekends.

Life was good.

Better than good.

I raised my red plastic cup. "To you guys. I'm so proud of what you've accomplished. It's— I'm not sure there's a word powerful enough to express how I feel right now. I'm happy to be a part of your foursome. Cheers." Everybody raised their cups or beer cans.

"Cheers."

"Can you play us something from your upcoming album?" Addison asked, taking the seat next to my girl.

"It's kind of embarrassing," Dahlia said.

Addison looked at her with one tipped brow. "C'mon, girl. Soon you'll play in front of thousands of people. Let us be your test run."

"Okay," Dahlia agreed, her cheeks an adorable shade of pink. She rose to get her guitar case from the back of my truck.

She sat back between my legs, next to Carter and Stud. They played "One More Night," and we all sang along. Most of us had heard the band practice that song dozens of times.

Then they played two more songs.

Pride and excitement filled the air. Carter and I fist-bumped, and he sauntered away toward his friends.

Dahlia put the guitar back in its case, and I pushed her copper hair over her shoulder to drop a kiss on her neck. The spot that sent shivers to her toes. Every single time. Her warmth transferred to my lips. My hands tightened around her waist.

"You'll do amazing out there, Princess. I know you will."

"This is bigger than anything I've ever dreamed of. I'm still not sure it's all real."

"Oh, believe me, it's happening."

Dahlia spun her head until our lips met. "I love you," she whispered against my mouth.

We lost ourselves in each other's gaze for a few beats before she brought her attention back to the bonfire.

My eyes traveled to all the people here to celebrate with us. Everyone had a smile pasted on. Behind the bushes, Carter and Phoenix were busy throwing a football. Addi was dancing with her boyfriend, country music playing from somewhere. Brendan joined us and clinked his beer bottle with Dahlia's red cup.

"You'll do great. I'm happy for you guys." They

exchanged a smile. "When you're rich and famous, don't turn your back on this dude," he said, pointing to me.

"Never." Dahlia flashed me a grin. "He's mine."

Ten minutes later, Brendan left us alone.

With my arms still wound around Dahlia's waist, I teased the skin of her neck with the tip of my tongue. She writhed against me, and my cock liked it a bit too much.

A soft moan escaped her mouth, and I was a goner. "Babe, I love you, but you'll kill me. Don't make that kind of noise in public."

She turned her head to face me. "I love you so much. Thanks for always having my back."

"Anytime, Princess."

My girl turned around and sank her body into mine, looping her arms around my neck.

Our tongues danced together, and I savored every corner of her mouth. The crotch of my pants tightened. Warmth rolled up and down my spine. Dahlia was the end of me. Anytime we were together, I lost track of everything else. Nothing in the world existed beside us. If soulmates happened, Dahlia was mine. Now. Here. And forever.

"I want to go back home with you," she whispered in my ear. My heart picked up its tempo.

"Dah—We can't. Your parents—"

Her hand curled around my hard-on. I gasped, trying to drive oxygen to my brain.

"Please, I want you. I'm ready for this."

"Baby, stop. I'll come in my pants. Oh—God— Princess—You're—"

My eyes searched Carter. He was laughing with Phoenix and Chris—Addison's boyfriend—further away. I blinked. This was the band's night. I had no intention of shoving my happiness in his face.

Dahlia rose to her feet and held out her hand for me to take.

I huffed and grabbed it, trying to hide my swollen cock from our friends. Dahlia pivoted until her back pressed to my front and swayed her hips, grinding her ass against my painful erection. Making it stiffer. And thicker.

My hands found her shoulders as I leaned forward. "Stop. Fine. We'll go home. Please stop. I'm begging you."

Her clear laughter broke something in me. A restraint I'd placed on myself months ago. The promise to never touch her that way before she was ready.

Our fingers intertwined, and I picked up Dahlia's guitar case from the ground, using it as a shield to hide the tent stretching the front of my pants. When we walked past Stud, I whispered into his ear. "Don't fucking come home before I text you. I'm not joking here. Don't you even dare, or I'm throwing you out."

Stud winked, a cocky smile taking over his face, but said nothing as he sipped his beer.

"Hey, Carter, don't drive home. I'll pick you up later, bro. Just wait for me," I almost screamed his way, my throbbing heart the only sound making it to my ears. The blood rushing to my dick rendered me lightheaded and breathless.

My brother gave me a thumbs-up, too distracted to care where I was going.

Some tension in my upper back left. I breathed easier.

Dahlia tugged at my hand, and I followed her, trying to swallow, as everything inside me tightened and pulsed.

Once in my truck, Dahlia's mouth attacked mine. She was fierce and gentle, hard and soft, all at the same time, leaving me no time to catch my breath. "Dah, wait—Are you sure?" I leaned back to meet her eyes.

"I've been ready for a while. You're always the one stopping it. I don't want to wait anymore."

"What about your dad? If we get caught, he'll kill me. I don't want to end up with a charge against me. You know he'll put me in jail."

"Stop talking about my daddy, Jeff," Dahlia said, biting my lower lip and shattering the last threads of my self-control. "I want you, and I know for a fact you want me. I can feel you. All of you." She dragged her fingernails down my chest. Her hand ventured lower until my thick length vibrated in her hand. "Yeah. I know you do. Stop arguing and bring me home."

I nodded, unable to speak. I looked at the time. We had two hours left before Dahlia's curfew. I would enjoy every second of it.

Once I pulled into my driveway and killed the engine, I circled the truck and opened the door to scoop Dahlia over my shoulder. Her laughter stoked the wildfire raging inside me. I fumbled with the door lock, my hands shaky.

"How many times have you done it?" she asked, her voice low, her teeth nibbling on my earlobe. Right now, long gone for her, I would've agreed to anything she asked for.

I dropped her to her feet and searched her eyes. "A few. Years ago. It meant nothing. I'm not sure I knew what love was before you. And I've loved nobody else but you, Princess." I tilted my head to graze her lips, soft and bright pink from all the kissing. "We don't need to do anything you're not comfortable with. We have all our lives to be together."

Dahlia rose to her toes. "I want to, Jeff. It's all I've been thinking about lately. Not the single playing on the radio. Not the record deal or the ton of money we were promised. All I want is you. No one else. Nothing else. The rest is just noise. Sure, it's fun, but you and I are all that matters. Please love me."

I cocked my head, studying my amazing girlfriend. Did she have any idea how bad she owned me? With her hair tied in a braid, her skinny jeans, black tank top, and cowboy boots, she looked every bit of gorgeous. Tonight, though, sex oozed from her. It was in her smile, the curves of her waist, the way she moved her hips. Dahlia grinned at me, grazing her lower lip, and my heart almost burst out of my chest.

"Fuck, I love you, Princess."

I scooped her over my shoulder again and brought her to the bedroom. The one that would be ours. Someday.

Dahlia lay on her back, my body hovering over hers, my fingers tangled in her hair. My lips cherished her jaw, neck, then her collarbone, and went back to her lips. She writhed underneath me, almost sending me to oblivion with only her touch.

"We can just kiss," I said, my voice low and gravelly, before crashing my lips on hers again. And again. Taking her mouth hostage, her tongue swirling against mine.

The room, lit only by the high moon shining through the window, cast a shadow of our entangled bodies on the wall. In the dim light, Dahlia's eyes sparkled. She stared at me as if I could do no wrong.

Her eyes bore into mine, and she snaked her arms around my back, keeping me close to her.

"No. I want it all. Tonight."

———

With my naked body pressed against Dahlia's soft chest, I drowned in her irises. They sucked me in. My body pulsated with so much need I ached to be inside her. To move to the rhythm of her hips. To let her consume me. But I was also afraid to hurt her. My mouth was dry, my breathing fast. The taste of her lingered on my lips. Her sweetness had woken all my senses and shattered me into millions of particles. How many times before did I dream about pleasuring her with my tongue? I'd stopped counting a long time ago.

Naked between my arms, Dahlia traced the length of my jawline with her finger. "Stop overthinking it. I'll be fine." Could she read my mind? "I'm ready. I don't want to wait anymore."

Her hand lowered between us and wrapped around my erection. I squirmed. And closed my eyes. My throat worked. My lips ate her, wanting to taste all of her again. There was no turning back now. I was long gone for the copper-haired girl who owned me, heart and soul. I delved one finger inside her.

"You're so wet, Princess."

"Because you turn me on. Oh—Yes. More. Gimme more."

I inserted a second finger inside her, stretching her, her walls tight around my digits. Dahlia rolled her hips, chasing her own pleasure.

"Do you want to stop?"

My girl shook her head. "No. Never."

"Then I think now you're ready."

I rose to my feet and hurried to the bathroom to fish out a condom. Straddling Dahlia's body, I sat on my heels to roll the rubber on. With her finger, she signaled me to come closer. She cast me under her spell. My eyes took in her naked flesh, ready to be cherished. My lips claimed hers with force. With love. With desire.

Carefully, I slid inside her warmth, giving her time to

adjust to me. Dahlia yelped and dug her nails in the skin of my shoulders.

I froze.

After a moment, I reclined to watch her.

"Are you all right?"

Dahlia opened her eyes, and she showered me with love.

"I've never been better. Please don't stop. Don't ever stop."

My tongue tasted the seam of her lips.

She moaned. I groaned.

And I slid back home where I belonged.

8

DAHLIA

I kicked the air as Jeff carried me over his shoulder, and I watched him as he fumbled with the door lock. Was I making him nervous?

He dropped me to my feet and studied me.

I cringed. Why did I ask him how many times he had sex before? It didn't matter. Jeff was mine. All mine. Why was I being weird?

"I'm not sure I knew what love was before you. And I've loved nobody else but you, Princess." He leaned over and skimmed my lips with his, shutting all the voices nagging me in my head. "We don't need to do anything you're not comfortable with. We have all our lives to be together."

His words sent my heart into overdrive.

He laid me down on his bed, his eyes trained on mine, and a small smile peeking at the corner of his lips. The opposite of the seriousness painting his face.

With steady hands, I peeled Jeff's T-shirt over his head and threw it on the floor, the pads of my fingers tracing the planes of his abs and chest muscles. I breathed fast. I tried to look casual, but an earthquake raged inside me. Ready to shatter my composure and fake confidence.

I wanted to pinch myself. This was finally happening.

We were still dressed—well, I was—and already my body could rip at the seams any second.

Jeff's lips landed on mine, stealing every bit of oxygen from my lungs. Lightheaded and breathless, I'd never felt so alive in my entire life. My body pulsed with need. Jeff and I had made out countless times, and our hands had ventured all over each other in the past, but right now, nothing compared to how I felt. My body had caught on fire, and I craved the burn. A whirlwind of sensations took over. Flutters danced in my lower belly. Goosebumps popped all over my skin. Warmth rippled the length of my spinal cord, kissing each vertebra. It turned me into a puddle in Jeff's skilled hands.

I hooked one leg around his lower back, craving the closeness of our bodies.

A growl escaped his mouth, and the tingling inside me increased.

His thick erection nested between my legs, and I gasped. How could our bodies fit so perfectly together? As if mine had been carved with the only purpose to fit his.

My boyfriend tilted his head back and looked at me—really looked at me—his eyes dark and overflowing with lust. Could he set me on fire with just his gaze? "You're beautiful, Princess. I love you. Tell me this isn't a dream."

My tongue darted out to run along my lower lip.

The room exploded in a rainbow of lights. My senses highlighted.

"I love you so damn much." My lips quivered. "Love me with all you've got."

A train of curses left Jeff's mouth. Then his lips claimed mine, ravaging my mouth.

Words I'd never dared to speak before swirled in my head. Sexy words. Dirty words. I couldn't get them out. When did I become sex-crazed? My hormones. Yeah, my hormones were to blame. Or Jeff's body as he ground against mine. Or his manly scent taking over all my senses. Or was it his hands clutching my waist? Jeff's lips traced a trail of kisses from my jaw to my collarbones, sucking, teasing, and licking my sensitive flesh. His mouth lowered down to the swelling of my breasts, sprinkling kisses over my skin, titillating my hard nipples with his teeth over the fabric of my shirt.

My back bucked off the mattress.

"Oh Jeff—"

Nothing had ever felt so good before.

"Princess, I'm addicted to the taste of you."

His eyes locked on mine, and jerking my hips to his, I let out a loud cry. A sound I never knew could escape my mouth.

One of Jeff's fingers traveled from my neck to the valley between my breasts, then to my belly button. My breath quickened—harsh and jerky—echoing his. Was he as aroused as I was?

I was a combusting bomb, ready to detonate. Jeff's hands slid under my shirt and bunched it around my ribcage. Holding on to my hipbones, he drew circles with his thumbs on my skin. His head dropped to my stomach, and with his tongue, he licked and kissed every inch of my bare flesh.

With my clothes burning my skin and getting in the way, I crossed my arms and gripped the hem of my tank top to take it off, leaving me exposed in my lilac cotton bra. Jeff's eyes darkened. His Adam's apple worked hard. He stared at me like a starving man.

Feeling self-conscious, I crossed my arms over my chest.

Jeff sat on his ankles, his heavy gaze never leaving me. In a sweet gesture, he uncrossed my arms and knitted our fingers together. "Never hide from me, Princess. I love every inch of you. Every cell. Everything about you is beautiful. You're beautiful."

All my restraints split open. Warmth spread inside me. I tried to clench my thighs as the desire between them became too hard to contain, but I couldn't move, having lost all control over myself. I squirmed on the bed, unable to breathe or swallow or even think.

With gentleness and fire in his eyes, Jeff unbuttoned my jeans and slid them down my legs. I watched him watching me.

The drumming of my heart vibrated through me.

Could he feel it too?

Without looking away from me, my boyfriend lowered his head to spread kisses from my knees up to my inner thighs. One leg, then the other. I fisted the sheets on either side of me, trying to stay put. His finger pulled the crotch of my panties to the side, and the tip of his tongue found my drenched center. The muscles of my jaw twitched. I tried to scream, but the sound died in my throat.

Shivers ran up and down my entire body.

The warmth of his mouth mixed with my wetness.

When Jeff sucked on my clit, I thought I would never come back from the rush.

He brought his finger to his mouth and licked the length of it. His eyes were now an ocean. Deep, dark, and bracing for a storm.

When he slid his digit inside me again, I gasped.

I rolled my head back, fisting the sheets harder.

Jeff had made me come with his fingers multiple times in the past, but his touch had never ignited my body like his mouth just did.

With my clit between Jeff's lips and his finger diving in and out of me, I lost contact with reality.

My body stiffened. I panted. A million sensations hit me at the same time. And I let go.

I rode the wave of pleasure, trying to even my breathing, to chase away the fog clouding my vision.

A slow grin appeared on my boyfriend's face. And I mirrored it because everything inside me was happy and bubbly. I wanted to smile like a fool. Dance like there was no tomorrow. Scream my love from the top of a mountain.

"Do you want to stop?"

Jeff's stare burned holes into my skin.

I bit my lower lip, shaking my head. "No. Never."

Jeff got to his feet, disappeared in the bathroom, and came back seconds later with a foiled square in his hands. He stopped a few feet from the bed, eyeing me with hunger and love.

I liquified at the sight of him.

The last thing I did before my boyfriend rocked my world with tenderness and passion was to beckon him with my forefinger. His lips crashed on my lips. His body fused with my body. We couldn't tell each other apart, our souls joined forever.

One hour later, under the covers, with our heads pressed together and our fingers intertwined, Jeff and I breathed the same air, our faces an inch apart. My heart was still begging to be freed. My flesh felt different. Sensitive. Ignited. Loved.

"Princess, I hate to say this, but I need to drive you home and pick Carter up. He must be wondering where we went. I can't believe I won't wake up with you in my arms in the morning."

I turned to my side and cradled Jeff's face in my hands. And kissed the tip of his nose.

His arm looped around my neck, and he pulled me to his chest.

When we broke apart, we both got dressed, the remnants of what we just shared lingering in the air.

"Let's get Carter," I said, thinking of my best friend, whom we left behind when we were supposed to celebrate our first single playing on the radio. Together. I sighed, a smile creeping onto my lips. Tonight, though, I'd had the best celebration I could ever ask for.

———

Four months later

I grabbed the key from under the doormat and let myself in. The house was silent. Only a nightlight was switched on in the kitchen, a star in the dark, showing me the way. In complete silence, I tiptoed to the bedroom. The sound of the shower got my pulse racing.

Not bothering to turn a lamp on, I undressed.

Heat billowed inside me.

I opened the bathroom door and peeked in. Steam filled the room. Jitters wiggled inside me.

I slid my naked body through the opening between the tiled white wall and the navy-blue shower curtain we'd picked out together. From behind, I wrapped my arms around Jeff's midsection and took a big whiff of his manly scent. Sandalwood and cinnamon. And soap. Jeff stepped forward, giving me access to the hot water stream. My lips trailed kisses between his shoulder blades. My tongue traveled down, licking and tasting my boyfriend's clean skin.

His body pulsated in my embrace.

Jeff turned on his heels and wound his arms around me.

"Hey," he said, his smile taking over his beautiful face, a day's long scrub darkening his jaw, the skin of his arms and chest golden, and his muscles leaner and more defined from working in construction.

"Hey yourself."

"Did you sneak out again?"

I nodded. "I had to see you. Between school, rehearsals, shows, and interviews, we barely ever spend time together anymore. I missed you."

Jeff traced the side of my face with his knuckles.

"I've missed you too, Princess. So much."

I pressed my head in his chest, welcoming his heart-beat, strong and steady, against my cheek. Jeff's erection saluted me, pressing hard against my lower belly.

"Hey you," I said, drawing my eyes down and curling my hand around his velvety flesh.

"He missed you too." Jeff smirked.

I worked him a few times, enjoying the throbbing inside my fist.

My tongue traced over his pec muscles.

"I'll crash here for a few hours, then I'll go back home. Carter helped me perfect my escape route. No one will notice I'm gone."

"You asked Carter to help you with this?"

"Yes. I didn't want to bring you into this. If Daddy ever finds out, you won't have to lie to him because you'll know nothing."

I scratched the side of my head.

"Guess it makes sense. You know you're as smart as you are hot, right?" His lips devoured mine. Time stopped. "Let's set some rules, though. No talking about my baby brother or your daddy when we're naked in the shower, Princess. Now turn around, I'll wash you." I obeyed. Jeff's large hands massaged my upper back, and I forgot about everything else.

Three months. And then no more hiding or sneaking out at night. *Three months*, I repeated in my head, letting all the sensations Jeff's closeness brought to my body take over.

9

JEFFREY

Five months later

"Are you serious right now?" Carter asked, his tone harsh, anger swimming in his gray eyes. "Why didn't you tell me?"

I dragged my hands over my face and sighed. I needed to have this conversation with my brother before breaking the news to my girl. "It's complicated, Cart. You wouldn't understand."

"C'mon, Jeff. Try me. You don't need to protect me. I'm not twelve anymore. You better have a good explanation." The muscles of his jaw flexed.

I slumped into the couch in our parents' garage—the same old stained couch that had been there forever—and hung my head low. "How can I explain without looking like a complete asshole? I want to do something meaningful with my life. You shine. I'm proud of you. And I'm proud of Dahlia too. But where does it leave me? I'm in your shadow, Cart. I want to be more than just the brother or boyfriend of two famous country music stars. When I say it like this, I sound lame—"

"I had no idea you felt this way." Carter dropped his tall self next to me and leaned forward, his elbows propped on his knees. He blew out a breath and shook his head. "I'm sorry, bro."

I raised my hands in surrender. "No, Cart. You did nothing wrong. I just need to figure out who I am on my own. The desire to find my own path has been nagging me for a while."

"Have you told her? You need to come clean. We're going away for almost a year. If you love her, be honest. Don't just throw it up in her face at the last minute."

"I will." I dipped my head lower, and Carter pulled me into a hug.

"I love you, big bro, but are you sure enlisting is the right thing to do? You've talked about this in the past, but I never thought you were serious about it."

I shrugged. "I won't know unless I try. But what if I could make a difference?"

Carter clapped my back. "I'll support you, no matter what, and you know it. But you have to promise me you'll always come back to us. Life would be too hard without my big brother around."

I nodded. "Same for you, Cart. Promise me you'll always come back home after each tour. I'll make it my mission to keep you grounded. I'll be your personal don't-let-fame-get-to-your-head coach."

Carter locked his arm around my neck, and we both laughed as we started wrestling. The same way we'd been doing for years. We rose to our feet and ended up on the floor. "You better get back in shape, brother, because right now, I'm kicking your ass. Big time," he teased.

"Yeah, yeah. Just shut up, man."

———

I forced my legs to run an extra mile. My entire body hurt. My muscles strained. My lungs burned. Running helped clear my mind. I told my brother I'd come clean, and I needed to relieve as much tension as possible before facing the girl owning my heart. The one who'd feel I let her down.

My back rested against the kitchen counter. I chugged my third glass of water. Dahlia stood before me, worry dancing in her moss-green eyes.

I breathed in and folded my arms over my chest.

"I need to tell you something." Her eyes widened, and she studied me, a deep wrinkle crossing her forehead. The pulse in her throat accelerated. A light flush crept over her cheeks. I cleared my throat. This was much harder than I thought it would be. "I—I enlisted."

All the color drained from her face.

"You what?"

"I enlisted, Princess. Three days ago."

Dahlia crossed her arms over her chest, mimicking my stance. A wall rose between us. "I heard you the first time. You didn't think of talking it over with me first? I thought we were a team." Hurt flashed in her eyes. I closed my eyes and sighed. "Why are you always making big life decisions before discussing them with me? First, college. Now, this. Why are you always leaving me in the dark, Jeff?"

Her tone was sharp.

A shiver ran through me.

"I thought you wanted an *us*, but it feels more like Jeff's one-man show right now." Her shoulders slouched in dismay, and my heart plummeted in my chest at the sight of her. "Why are we even having this conversation if you've already made up your mind? You don't need my input, so do whatever you want. I won't get in your way."

She spun on her heels and ran away. Seconds later, she slammed our bedroom door. I was an idiot. I had no idea what to do right now. Beg Dahlia to let me in and figure this out together, or drive away and give her some space.

My throat clenched.

My breathing hitched.

I ran a hand over my face.

I blew out a breath and walked toward the hallway leading to our bedroom. Inhaling some courage in, I knocked on the door. "Princess, let me in. I'm sorry. I never meant to hurt you." I rested my forehead against the door. "I've been thinking about this for a while. You know, I already told you. But that morning, three days ago, you'd gone to rehearsal, and I felt like I needed to do something big. You and Carter have this whole life figured out, and I'm stuck in mine. I know we're still young, but I want my life to mean something too." I sighed, my forehead still pressed against the wooden panel. "I love our lives together, but I need to find my place in this world. I want to help. Change things. I'm fortunate in life. It's my time to give back. To try something new. I can't be the guy following you around the globe like a pathetic puppy. I'm sorry, Princess. You're right. I should've told you. I know it's big. I'm sorry. Let me in—Please. I need you. I'll always need you."

I shut my eyes, trying to chase my tears away. Was I being selfish?

I snorted and rubbed my nose with the back of my hand.

I stayed there for a long time, listening to the bursting of my heart.

Maybe Carter was right. Maybe I could have picked

another career. I loved working in construction. And I was good at it. The thoughts in my head raced until I grew lightheaded.

Just when I was about to crumple on the floor, Dahlia opened the door. Sadness defined her red-rimmed eyes. Her bottom lip quivered.

"Hey," I said. "Can we talk?"

Dahlia snorted and shook her head. "I don't want to talk. Not right now. I love you. Nothing will change that. But you've hurt me. A lot. I feel like I mean nothing to you. Like my voice has no weight—"

I cradled her face. "You know that's not true, Princess."

She looked down. "Is it? You always shut me out. Why? I can deal with whatever you have to tell me. Stop treating me like I need your protection. I'm going on a freaking world tour. I need to be able to fend for myself. I need you to trust me to do that."

My lips brushed hers. "I trust you, and I know you can take care of yourself. I don't want to keep anything from you. I'm sorry I did. Never again. I'll be more considerate next time." Dahlia wrapped her arms around my midsection and rested her face on my chest. My heart became whole again.

We stood there, in our bedroom doorway, breathing each other in, our hearts healing together.

After a long minute, Dahlia pushed back. "Since we won't see each other a lot in the next year, we better make the most of our last month together." Some of the tension in my back drew away. The lump blocking my throat disintegrated.

"Are we okay?"

Dahlia's eyes lit up. A little. "Yes. We need to be. Let me wrap my head around it, then we'll talk." I kinda smiled, grazing her lips with mine. "You know the best way to get over a fight, right?" Her lips curved up, and she winked at me, trying hard to hustle her pain away. I saw it in her eyes.

"I love how you think, woman." I stepped back and tugged at her hand. "C'mon, then. I desperately need a shower right now. Care to join me?"

I removed my shirt.

"You know I can't resist you." Dahlia scrunched up her nose. "Those abs of yours are really hard to say no to."

I chuckled. "Then there's no reason for you to protest." I offered her my best panties-melting grin, and without a word, she shimmied out of her black leggings.

I lifted my girl in my arms, and she hooked her legs around my waist. My mouth claimed hers. She entangled her fingers in my hair. "Everything will be all right, Princess. I promise."

Still damp and naked, we clung to each other as we entered the kitchen. The sun had set, and through the window, we watched the sky, now a painting of orange and pink stripes. I tightened my grip around my girlfriend. If only we could stay like this forever.

"I didn't know you felt that way," she said, breaking the comfortable silence. "Carter and I have always tried to make you feel like you were part of our band." Dahlia tilted her head back until it rested in the crook of my neck.

"It's not your fault. You did nothing wrong. Don't ever blame yourself. It's all on me. I need to see where this thing is going to take me."

Dahlia nodded, and we stood like that for the next half hour, watching as the day faded and darkness settled in.

10

DAHLIA

J eff pulled Carter into a hug, "Go shine, brother. You were born for this," he said, and they both clapped each other's backs. My boyfriend turned to face me, and I hurried into his arms. "Princess, you'll be amazing up there. Look at me." I tilted my head back. "I'm so proud of you." He tucked a strand of hair behind my ears.

I rose to my tiptoes. "I love you."

With the pads of his fingers, he wiped the tears pooling in the corners of my eyes.

"I love you too."

I looked around. "It's kinda scary. All those people. The stage, the crowd—"

"Carter will be up there with you. You have nothing to worry about."

Riley stepped next to us. "Okay, Dahlia, time to go. Ready?"

"I guess."

Would my voice be shaky like this on stage?

Butterflies took flight in my stomach. The not-so-fun kind.

I walked away, my hand locked in Jeff's, touching until our fingers broke apart.

Carter neared me and snaked his arm through mine. "It's okay, Dah. I'm here. We can do this. Just follow my lead, I'll take care of everything."

Those words.

My pulse evened.

We exchanged a smile as Stud padded in our direction and put his arms around us.

"Let's show them what we've got." He stopped and pulled us into his embrace. "We're kicking off our first world tour. How awesome is that? Let's do this, mother-fuckers."

Stud's longish stubble rapped my cheek.

"Oh yes," Carter said as I replied, "Let's make history."

The lights of the stage blinded me. My heart sank down to my toes. "Seventy thousand people," I said, mostly to myself. "Seventy thousand."

My insides tightened. Carter said a few words to the crowd, but I registered none. My eyes drifted to the right side where Jeff stood. Did I look like a deer caught in head-lights? My fingers shook. My head turned. My legs wobbled. I tried to breathe, but my lungs were closed for business.

"You can do this," Jeff mouthed.

I swallowed the lump choking me.

Carter strummed the first chords of "Heart for Rent." My heart leaped in my throat. Why did I agree to this? I loved our simple garage band. This, right here, was way too big for a White Crest girl like me. I shut my eyes, silencing my thundering heart. I could do this. I breathed

out. My fingers played on their own. I locked my eyes on
my best friend. He winked. No one was here except the
two of us—and Stud. We were back in Carter's garage,
dreaming about getting fifty people to come see us play.

This—right here—was our dream.

I rolled my shoulders—chasing the tension away—
rotated my neck and found my voice.

We played for ninety minutes, but it seemed like we
played for fifteen.

The crowd cheered, whistled, and applauded.

My heart swelled, and my pulse quickened.

Carter and Stud pulled closer and, standing on either
side of me, grabbed my hands.

Carter turned his head. "We did it, Dah," he whispered in my ear, the warmth of his breath tickling the shell
of my ear. I cocked my head to meet his gaze. Everything
we wanted to say to each other passed through our eyes.
His were a silver shade of gray tonight and full of stars.
Carter's lips connected with my temple.

"We did it," I repeated as I emptied all the air lodged
in my lungs.

With his hand, Carter motioned Jeff to join us onstage.
And Riley. My man stood between his brother and me, his
arms draped around our shoulders. Riley stood beside
Stud.

"That was incredible," Jeff said.

"Yes, it was," Carter said, his smile big and bright.

The next day, still reeling from the previous night's
show, we packed our stuff and boarded the tour bus that
would drive us to Portland, San Francisco, LA, and Las
Vegas—the first leg of our world tour. Then we'd fly to
Canada, Europe, and Asia, before coming back to the US
for another two months.

———

"Did you pack my blue dress?" I asked Jeff as he sat on my overflowing suitcase, trying to zip it up. "I don't remember doing it, and I can't find it anywhere." My breathing picked up as I scanned the room. Our bedroom.

We'd been living together for four months now. Everything in my life now made perfect sense. At eighteen, it felt like I had found all my purposes. Could it be so, or was I too inexperienced to see the complete picture?

Moisture filled my eyes.

My breath quivered in my lungs.

The emotional chaos inside me couldn't be contained much longer.

In a few hours, I'd be leaving for Vancouver. We came back from our show in Las Vegas one week ago. The second leg of our first world tour was about to start. From the moment our first single reached the top spot on the charts, we'd become the new country music sensation. We'd given more interviews in the last year than I even thought possible. We'd already played a dozen shows all over the country. Jeff had been following us as much as he could, sometimes flying overnight just to see us play or spend time with me. And I loved him even more each time.

The thought of being away from White Crest for almost a year tightened my stomach.

My family lived here.

My life was here.

And this was where my heart belonged.

I swallowed, trying to prevent my emotions from stirring inside me.

My angst wasn't all due to me going on tour.

"When are you leaving?" I asked, my heart flickering.

Jeff inhaled, and his Adam's apple bobbed. He sighed

and lowered his head, keeping his chin close to his chest. For a minute—a very long minute—he said nothing. Then he raised his eyes and gazed at me. "In two days. I'll be gone for a little over three months. I'm sorry I'll miss so many shows. You know I wish I could follow you on the road and overseas, but—" His voice faltered.

I straddled him and squeezed his hands in mine.

"We'll be okay. We're both aiming for our goals. But promise me that when you're shipped out to somewhere dangerous, you'll stay safe and come back to me. Always. That's all I'm asking. That you come back to me. Every. Single. Time. Alive. And in one piece. Not a casket."

A lone tear rolled down my cheek.

Jeff leaned closer to kiss it off.

His lips brushed mine.

My heart jumped in my throat, an invisible clamp strangling it.

"I'll come back to you, Princess. I promise. You're my life. My destiny. My future." His eyes turned gloomy. His voice shook. "Please, Dah, take care of my baby brother for me. Keep an eye on him. I don't want this new fame thing to kill his soul. Make sure he stays grounded."

"Jeff, it's Carter. He's stronger than all of us. I trust him with my life. But I'll always be there for him. Until we're all gray and old."

Jeff's lips quirked up.

"You'll be a gorgeous old lady." We both burst into a fit of laughter, and it erased some of the tension in the air. "And I've asked Cart to watch over you too. Just so you know."

A small smile grazed my lips.

"Are you afraid fame will change me?" I arched one brow, waiting for his explanation.

"No. But you'll meet all kinds of nasty people out

there. And there'll be drugs. And all sorts of stuff I prefer not to think about. I just want you to be safe."

"God, you're hot when you're all protective. Carter and I will have each other, but who's gonna look out for you?"

"I'm a big boy, Princess. As long as I know you two are safe, I'll watch over me, myself. Don't worry about me. Do what you have to do. Reach for your dreams, then we'll meet up here. Always."

A flow of tears streamed down my face. I had everything I'd always wished for since I was a little girl right here in the palm of my hand. When did I get so lucky in life?

My hands cupped Jeff's cheeks as he kissed my tears—and my pain and worries—away.

I unbuttoned his shirt with shaky fingers. Butterflies took off deep inside me.

Jeff gripped the hem of my shirt and peeled it off me.

Our mouths crashed in a dance we'd rehearsed an infinite number of times. We took everything from each other, then gave it all back, a million times bigger and brighter.

Jeff leaned back.

"To answer your question, I packed the blue dress after I picked it up from the dry cleaner yesterday. It's in your red bag."

My lips landed back on his, hungrier and wilder.

Jeff tore each piece of clothing off me.

Our skin met, hot and sweaty, needy for each other's touch. I memorized each inch of him. I had no idea when we'd be together again. Somehow, it felt like the last time. I imprinted myself in his scent. I carved his skin with my fingernails, etching myself on him.

I kissed his jaw, neck, his chest and lowered myself down his body until I could taste the very last inches of him. Jeff vibrated inside my mouth. He groaned. I moaned. His fingers fisted my hair, setting the pace. My tongue twirled around the tip of his cock as I pumped the base with my hand. His body stiffened.

"God, Dah, I can't believe we won't be able to do this for months—" I sucked harder, stealing his ability to form words away.

Our gazes met. The back of my eyes burned with unshed tears at the thought of being apart for so long.

Tears I refused to cry for now, not willing to spoil this moment between us.

My heart bled. Everything in me became a blaze. A flame of desire and love. And a fire of pain and goodbyes.

"Don't cry, Princess," Jeff said, pulling me toward him. "Don't cry."

My man laid me on my back as if I were made of feathers. His hands found my breasts, and he kneaded them, molding them to fit his hands. He pinched my diamond-hard nipples.

I let out a loud cry.

A cry of love. Of loss. Of fear. Of pleasure.

His tongue teased the flesh under my earlobe, making its way down to my wet and throbbing center. Every fiber in me screamed his name. Screamed to be touched. To be loved. I needed him to singe himself into me.

Jeff's tongue flicked over my clit as his fingers entered me. Slowly at first, then with purpose. To shatter me into a million pieces and build me back into a more powerful version of myself.

My boyfriend ravaged me with his tongue. Pleasure, simmering deep inside me, surfaced as his fingers dived in and out of me at a frenzied pace. I rolled my head back as heat washed over me. Jeff's tongue entered me, and everything went black. My body trembled. I breathed out in quick jolts.

"Jeff—" I screamed his name, and he swallowed my

gasps, his lips over mine, with the promise that everything would be all right.

When he unrolled a condom over his length, I squirmed on the mattress.

I hated the idea Jeff had enlisted in the Army. I'd never thought he'd go through with this. I thought he loved his job. And that he wouldn't risk his life for some grand life ideal. But he'd always supported my dreams, and I'd forever support his. No matter how they pricked my heart like a million needles.

Jeff thrust in and out of me. I felt him everywhere. Inside and outside of me. The electricity in the room could light up a stadium. We were combusting together. Two poles of a magnet coming together. Uniting. And exploding.

Jeff fastened his grip on my hips as he rammed into me. Hard and fast.

It was the heartbreak of being apart. It was love. It was a promise to always find our way back to each other.

My body tensed as I came undone.

The orgasm broke me.

It burned me down to ashes.

Jeff reached his own release and collapsed over me, clutching me against him as if he feared I'd vanish. Our tears mixed. We said nothing. This was the beginning, but it felt like the end.

Jeff's mouth fused with mine. Our tongues entangled together in a slow dance. Saying everything we hadn't said out loud. I anchored myself to my boyfriend, scared to walk away. Scared to let him go.

"We'll be okay, Princess. We'll be okay. It's you and me."

"It's you and me," I echoed. "You and me."

Sobs rocked my body, and I focused on Jeff's heartbeat as he loved me all over again.

Hours later, Carter picked me up, and Jeff and he stacked my luggage into the trunk of the car Riley sent. We all hugged one another. I was waiting for the excitement to kick in. It would. I knew it would. But not right now. I needed some time to grieve.

"I'll always love you, Princess. Never forget that." Jeff dropped a kiss on my forehead, and Carter held my hand, leading me away.

I didn't even remember getting into the car that brought us to the airport.

I knew our lives would never be the same.

I spent the entire ride nested in my best friend's arms, sobs rocking through me.

I couldn't wait to chase my dreams.

But I couldn't wait to be in Jeff's embrace again, in the safety of his arms.

And his love.

Eight months later

I knocked on Carter's hotel suite door. It was past two o'clock in the morning. He yanked the door open, his dark hair—now longer—disheveled, and his eyelids heavy with sleep. "Another nightmare?" he asked as he raked his fingers through his locks, messing it up even more.

I nodded and jumped into his arms, only to realize he was bare-chested. His warmth shot through me. Carter's arms wrapped around my back. He was my safe haven. Always had been.

"Talk to me, Dah."

I snorted and rubbed the heels of my hands over my eyes.

"It's Jeff. I haven't had any news from him in almost five weeks. What if something happened to him? What if he's hurt somewhere in the desert and nobody comes to his rescue, or he has amnesia? What if—?"

Carter clamped my upper arms. "Stop. Enough. If something had happened to him, we'd know by now." He stepped back and laced his fingers through mine. "C'mon. You need to sleep. You can't keep worrying like this. It's unhealthy." He tipped my chin up with a finger. "When was the last time you slept through the night?" I shrugged. "Tell me. I'm pretty sure I know the answer anyway."

"Fine. Since he'd been deployed. I can't even—" Sobs rocked through me. My entire body quivered. Carter knew all about my nightmares—I'd been coming to his room in the middle of the night a few times a week for months now.

My best friend led me to his bedroom. In the dark, he slid his legs into a pair of gray sweat shorts and fished a black T-shirt from a suitcase. Then he erased the distance between us and blanketed me in his strong arms before kissing the crown of my head.

"I'm sorry for bothering you, Cart."

"Shhh." He flipped the covers of the bed and motioned me to climb in. "Sleep it off. We'll talk in the morning." I hauled myself into the king-sized bed.

"Thanks."

"Anytime, Dah. I'm glad we have each other to go through this. I hate knowing Jeff is in danger as much as you do. Night."

"Night, Carter."

In a death grip, I held his hand in mine and drifted to sleep.

Whatever would happen in my life, my friendship with Carter was something I'd cherish forever. He still had feelings for me—I was well aware—but we talked about it and found a safe balance where we could be there for each other without things being awkward between us. Carter knew where my heart stood, and I loved him even more for not asking anything more from me than what I could give him.

11

JEFFREY

A year later

"You can't talk to me this way," Dahlia stated, rage slicing her words.

"I'm not doing anything wrong here. Stop trying to start a fight with me. Am I not allowed to be mad once in a while? I guess I never got the memo if that's how things are supposed to be. Do you need me to act as if rainbows are coming out of my ass twenty-four-seven? Is that it? You can't be serious, Princess. That's a freaking joke. Did the world tour mess with your head?" I huffed.

"Don't 'Princess' me." Dahlia looked at me with anger swimming in her eyes. If only looks could kill, I'd be dead. Once and for all.

My girl didn't get it. Nobody did. She and Carter thought they were smartasses, but they had no idea. I didn't need them to fix me. There was nothing to fix. Dahlia clenched her fists and rested them on her hips.

"I've never asked you to be Mr. Sunshine but only to paste a smile on your face once in a while. I'm sure what you went through was hard. Painful. And even devastating. But how could I know? You never talk to me anymore. You tell me nothing. You disappear in your stupid garage every time you're upset, which is most of the time, or you drink half a bottle of whiskey when you can't sleep. You spend all your time locked in here. So don't tell me I'm clueless. You're the one who is choosing to keep me in the dark."

A bright red flush crept along her cheeks. Her green eyes darkened as she studied me.

I punched the kitchen wall, making a dent in the drywall.

"Go, ahead. Keep acting like this. It's much better. Charming even." Dahlia brought her hands over her face and took a big intake of air as she shook her head. "Jeff, you need help. Professional help. And I'm saying this because I love you. Your entire family is worried about you too. Since you don't want my help, then find someone else. I'm sure the Army can provide you with a psychologist or someone—"

My voice rose. I spewed fury. "And you think a shrink will erase all the fucking images flashing in my mind all the time? Like he'll wave his magic wand, and everything will be forgotten? Yeah, right. Keep dreaming. I didn't think you still believed in fairy tales, Princess." I breathed out and dropped the sarcasm. With a lowered voice, I added, "It doesn't matter if I'm asleep or awake. Those images just won't go away."

Dahlia's face smoothed, and she closed the distance between us. She pulled my fists into her hands and opened them. One at a time—I hadn't even noticed my hands were clenched. "I'm here. I'll always be here. If you wanna talk, I'll listen. Don't keep it all to yourself, okay?" I hung my head and nodded. "Now let's do something together. In two months, I'll go back on our second world tour, and our lives will get crazy again."

My eyes filled with unshed tears. How did I become so bitter? Joining the Army was supposed to help me change the world, not destroy mine. How was my girl still by my side after all these months? I'd been a mess since I came back from the Middle East. I choked on my breathing just thinking about it. I couldn't put what I'd experienced into words. None of it happened the way it should have. Those women died. My hands trembled. My pulse picked up. Beads of cold sweat popped on my nape. I cocked my head to stare at my girl.

"I need you, Dah." My voice was shaky. "I'll always need you. I'm sorry for shutting you out. One day, I'll let you in. Gimme some time."

I fisted her hair and crashed my mouth on hers as if her love could save the remnants of hope lingering somewhere inside me. Dahlia looped her arms around my neck and sank her body into mine. The feeling of her boobs pressed against my chest sent bolts of electricity down to my dick. Our tongues danced together in a messy kiss, both of us yearning for each other.

"Fuck." I lifted her black sweater over her head and yanked her yoga pants and panties down her legs. Her braless tits stared at me, their tips pink and puckered. "Turn around." Dahlia spun on her heels and braced herself against the kitchen table—the one we'd recycled when I first bought the house years ago. My woman had made more money than she could ever have dreamed of by now, but we were still living in our DIY house. Because for us, it was home. We needed nothing more.

I dipped one finger into her wet center and soon added a second one, stretching her tight channel. Dahlia yelped. I spread her moisture all over her folds, and she shivered as my thumb circled her clit. From behind, I eased into her in one thrust. Dahlia melted in my arms. She arched her back, and I curled an arm around her bare chest. Her tits bounced every time I rammed into her.

My girl lowered her head and sucked my thumb into her mouth. She twirled her tongue around my digit before biting it. It stung. But the flicker of pain made me even harder for her. Heat rippled along my spine. My balls tightened. Dahlia stiffened in my embrace. She let go of my thumb, and my hand traveled down her body to grab a handful of her breast, kneading it to fit my hand. A low, guttural growl tumbled out of my mouth as I pounded into her a few more times. My vision blurred. I saw stars as I shot my load deep inside her. Dahlia came hard, her body quivering against mine. We both surfed our climaxes. Once the pleasure dissipated, she relaxed between my arms.

We stayed like this for a minute, trying to catch our breaths.

Dahlia broke the silence first. "I needed this. I needed to connect with you."

I peppered kisses on the moist skin between her shoulders, then linked them with the tip of my tongue, enjoying the saltiness of her flesh.

I sighed.

The ball of fury inside me had dissolved.

Dahlia always had this effect on me. Each time we found each other—after one of our storms—she soothed my troubled mind and everything else inside me. If only I could find a way to let her in. But I refused to let her see my demons. How much the war had damaged me. The images haunting me were mine. Dahlia didn't need to share them. They were mine to tame. Mine to overcome. Never would I be willing to corrupt her pure soul.

"Come here." I turned Dahlia and pulled her into my

arms. "Let's take a shower. I want to make love to you this time. To cherish every inch of your body. I'm sorry for being a mess. It has nothing to do with you. You're the light keeping me going. I love you."

My lips feasted on hers.

Everything around us vanished.

I needed to find a way to come back to the woman I loved. To be the man she deserved.

"I love you," she said against my mouth.

And my heart swelled in my chest, lighter than it'd been for months.

Our souls fused together, and for a few hours, I knew I'd feel like the old Jeff. The guy I missed so damn much and feared I'd never be again.

When we kissed, it chased away the cloud of darkness around my heart, and we were back to being the teens in love we'd been years ago. Having an insatiable desire for each other. After all, we had over a year to make up for. So many promises to fulfill and wounds to heal.

Then morning came, and everything inside me darkened.

My heart turned to stone.

And my mind flew back to the war.

Again.

12

DAHLIA

I woke up to the scent of pancakes and grits. My mouth watered. I touched the sheets beside me. They were cold. Propped on my elbows, I scanned the bedroom. No trace of my man.

Things had been smooth between us in the last month. Better. Much better. We'd been surfing a wave of calm, and hope had taken root inside me. Just thinking about it made me giddy. And it sent a grin to my face.

"Good, you're awake," Jeff said as he entered the room with a tray in his hands. "Made you breakfast, Princess. Hope you're hungry." He flashed me a smile. One that transformed me into a puddle of mush. His eyes shone as he drew the drapes open.

"Starving." Jeff placed the tray in front of me. Blueberry pancakes. Orange juice. Grits. Half a grapefruit. And a single red rose. My stomach grumbled as if it agreed with me.

"You did all this?"

"Yeah. And you haven't seen anything yet."

I bunched my brows together. "Tell me."

"Not a chance. It's a surprise."

I tugged at the hem of his black T-shirt, pulling him toward me, and batted my eyelashes.

"Please." I used my sultriest voice. Jeff pinched his lips together and shook his head.

"No. Forget it. I'm not telling you. Eat. You'll need all the strength you can get later." His lips brushed mine, and my heart hiccupped. He leaned back, his tone now husky. "Come, join me when you're done." He exited the room only to come back seconds later. "And by the way, forget your morning shower. It'll have to wait." He winked. Heat pooled in my lower belly. What did he do this time? I still stared at the doorway minutes after he disappeared, wondering what my boyfriend had planned.

Last weekend, he'd prepared a picnic, and we spent the afternoon in Milwaukee Park, cuddling on a blanket, watching kids fly kites.

I dressed in ripped-at-the-knees blue denims and an off-the-shoulder white cotton shirt and tiptoed into the kitchen, trying to spy on Jeff's secret project. I heard a table saw going in the garage, so perhaps we would build a terrace in the backyard or a new shelf for the living room.

I yanked open the door leading to the garage. My eyes widened.

Jeff's pickup truck cargo bed was filled to the brim with wood planks and boxes.

The sight of my boyfriend, shirtless with his muscular back glistening with sweat, emptying the contents on the garage floor, sent electric bolts through me.

My tongue swept my bottom lip as I admired him.

Each day, he looked more and more like the version of him I grew to love. The storm in him was still brewing, but it had decreased to a containable category-two hurricane instead of a ruining-everything-in-its-passage category-five tornado.

I cleared my throat. "Hey. Will you tell me what we're building today?"

Since the day Jeff bought the house, we'd spent countless hours doing all kinds of DIY projects together. It was a passion we shared, and we were good at it.

Jeff pivoted on his heels until he faced me. "Hey, Princess. How long have you been standing there?" I shrugged. "I have a whole day planned, but if you keep ogling me like this, we won't get anything done." He tipped one eyebrow, and I sighed before returning his smile.

I firmed my back. "Okay. I'll stop. If you promise to never put a shirt on. A girl needs some fantasy to get through her day."

Jeff strode my way and held out his hand. "Fine. We have a deal." I shook his hand, but he didn't let go and pulled me to his hard chest, rubbing his sweaty skin against me, his hands tickling my waist, his laughter contagious.

I pushed back, my lips fixed into a permanent smile. "Okay, what's the plan? I can't wait to get started."

"You know this out-of-this-century room we call a bathroom? We're stripping it down to its studs and building it back up. I got the black tiles you love so much," he said, pointing to the white boxes lined up on the floor next to his truck, "and referred to the vision board you sent me a while back for the rest. I hope it's all right with you." Jeff gazed at me with a lopsided smile.

My heart danced in my chest.

I jumped into his arms and looped my arms around his neck.

"You're kidding, right? It's perfect. Ohmygod. I love you so much right now."

Jeff spun me around before putting me back down. "Let's get to work then."

———

One week later

"I thought we've made progress. I guess I was wrong. What is going on? Can't you just stop?" I yelled, massaging the base of my neck to relieve some tension. This couldn't be the end of us. Tears flowed down my face. I huffed. Fighting all the time was exhausting. I pushed some of my anger away and walked to him across the living room, but Jeff stepped back. There was something in his eyes. A dark shadow. Something I'd never seen before. Was it pain or something else? Jeff would never do anything to hurt me. I knew that. But right now, I feared he'd hurt himself.

Without a word to me, he cut across the kitchen and hurried into the garage, slamming the door behind him. I followed him, but stopped at the door, needing a few minutes to calm down. I leaned my forehead on its flat surface, tears falling down my cheeks, and hoped my love could make its way to his heart. What was happening to us? All of a sudden, my body couldn't seem to stand straight.

I slid down the door and rested my head on my folded knees.

Bam. Bam. "You stupid shit." *Bam. Bam, bam, bam.*

The entire house vibrated. What was that? I jumped to my feet and entered the garage.

In the doorway, I froze. The scene playing in front of me wrecked my heart. And my soul.

Jeff was throwing cans of paint all over the place. The silver concrete floor was covered in a spectrum of colors.

Blue. Yellow. Red. Black. A shelf was tipped to the side, and a bottle of whiskey was shattered at his feet. I blinked twice, assessing the extent of the damage.

Jeff didn't acknowledge my presence. He kept throwing things around, restless. I'd never seen him like that. He looked possessed. As if someone had taken over his body.

I strode in his direction. "Easy. We don't need to talk. Put that down," I said in a low voice, removing a can of wood dye from his hand.

"I can't. I need to erase those images from my head. I can't take it anymore." He snorted and slid the back of his hand under his nose. Was he crying? I couldn't tell. Too many emotions etched his face. His bloodshot eyes looked empty. His lips trembled.

I had no idea what triggered today's meltdown. My man woke up in a bad mood and threw a fit before I was even up.

A mask of pain took over his face.

My Jeff was locked somewhere inside this man, but I couldn't reach him.

"They stoned them, Dah. And there was nothing we could do—nothing I could do. I watched all these women die. I enlisted to help and never felt so helpless."

I fastened my arms around his shuddering body as sobs rocked through him. I stood there, my heart broken into a million pieces, my stomach tied into a string of knots, acid simmering down my throat.

Jeff's shoulders heaved, and he pulled away, sitting on the floor, his back resting against the wall, his hands over his ears, and his eyes shut.

The sight of him, looking like a little child, broke everything in me.

I hugged myself with my arms.

A stream of tears flew down my cheeks.

Pain. Sadness. Helplessness.

Lost in my own head, trying to come up with ways to salvage what was left of my relationship with the man who stole my heart years ago, I didn't hear Carter coming through the side door.

He tugged my hand until I rested against his chest. "What happened this time?" I dried my tears with my fingertips and shrugged.

"I don't know. He started screaming. He hadn't slept in a few days."

Carter looked around, taking in the chaos surrounding us. "I thought he was doing better," he said.

Our eyes landed on my man in his own world, not paying us any attention.

"I did too. Now I don't know what to think. We're leaving in two weeks—"

"He needs help."

The air in the room, heavy and tense, suffocated me.

My heart bled. Jeff had raised a thick, high wall around him, and I lacked ways to climb over it.

Carter and I busied ourselves cleaning up the mess as Jeff sat there, his gaze empty. As he if was thousands of miles away from here.

From across the room, my eyes found Carter's. *Are you okay?* they asked.

Yeah. I don't know what to do, mine answered back as they drifted to Jeff.

My best friend inched closer.

"You want me to talk to him?"

"What's the point? He just wants to be left alone. Guess what? His wish will be granted. We're leaving for South America, and he'll have all the space he needs." A heaviness settled in my chest. As much as I ached for my boyfriend, I was also tired of all this. "Maybe some time apart is what we both need."

I wiped off the new set of tears building up in my eyes with the sleeve of my teal shirt—Jeff's favorite color on me.

"Can I at least try?" Caster asked me, a little spark in his eyes.

"Go ahead." I turned on the balls of my feet and stormed inside the house.

With my back resting against the door, I clamped my hands together to stop the tremors. I heard the voices on the other side.

Carter said something I didn't quite catch.

"…I'd never hurt her. I love her, man. I'd be dead if it weren't for her. Never say I don't deserve her ever again. When I was in the middle of the fucking desert, the thought of seeing her again was the only thing keeping me alive. Don't talk to me about relationships when you have none. You have no idea what you're talking about."

Carter spoke in a low voice, and I heard nothing.

"Dahlia's mine. It's about time you accept that, little bro. Let us deal with our own shit. None of it concerns you. Stop pining over my girl. Get a life. Stop living through ours."

A loud pound resonated in the garage.

"Go to hell, big bro. That's low. You used to be considerate. Now you're nothing but an angry jerk."

The sound of something shattering startled me. I wanted to go in there, but I couldn't, my feet glued to the kitchen floor.

"Leave my girl alone. We don't need you, Carter."

"Who do you think has to step up every time you step down? Who was there for her when you were trying to prove a point by joining the Army? It was me. Every time. So don't you tell me what I should or shouldn't do. You brought this on you. Screw you. I came here to talk to you, not to be blamed for caring for the girl I'd give my life for but who chose you and loves you enough to deal with all your shit—"

"She loves me. Not you. Why can't you accept it?"

"You knew how I felt about her when you asked her out. You never took my feelings into consideration. That was a low blow. You fucking broke me that day. We were supposed to have each other's back—" Carter's voice cracked.

Jeff mumbled something inaudible from where I stood.

I cupped my mouth with both hands.

I ran to my bedroom, choking on my sobs.

I stripped down, removing all my clothes from my body as if they had caught fire.

I jumped into the shower, wishing the hot water would ease my pain.

———

An hour later, I sat at the kitchen table, listening to sad country songs, a cup of tea in front of me, one leg folded, my arm wound around it. My eyes traveled across our small house. The cream kitchen cabinets Jeff and I repainted together when he moved in because they were a dull shade of nugget-yellow before. The worn-out hardwood floor. The red pillows sprinkled on the L-shaped couch. The black and white photo of Carter, Jeff, and me on prom night that I framed by the fireplace.

Would I ever be able to walk away from this life?

An emptiness replaced the parcels of joy inside me.

I sighed and pushed my shoulders forward.

Carter entered the house and joined me.

I cocked my head to stare at him. "How did it go?"

My best friend made himself a cup of tea and took a seat beside me, giving me a shrug. "I think he finally listened. But he's in denial. I'm not sure he understands how bad this is." He shook his head and exhaled.

"What did you tell him? Wait. You don't have to tell me. It's none of my business. Anyway, I heard too much already."

"Fuck. I'm sorry. I didn't know you were—I didn't mean to—"

My best friend squeezed my hand, and my body relaxed under his touch.

I wasn't ready to deal with every confession I heard earlier. "We don't have to talk about it, Cart. Some other time maybe. Not today."

Carter bowed his head. "Fine." He sipped his tea, avoiding my eyes. When he brought his attention back to me, he spoke in a low voice. "I told him he needs to get a grip on himself and seek help. That he needs to make a choice. Get his shit together or he'll end up miserable and alone."

"Do you think he'll agree?"

"I don't know. He listened. Perhaps it's a start. Oh, and you need to pack him a bag."

My eyes flared. "Wait. Why?"

"I'm bringing him home with me. You can't hold the burden all on your own, Dah. It's too much. I'll bring him back in a few days. Get some time off. Call Addi. Go to a spa or whatever you girls do when you're together. It'd be good for you. You've already done enough."

A lump formed in my throat, my emotions pushing to get through. "You're sure?" Carter nodded. "This could be fun." Why was he always so selfless around me? Somedays, I wondered what I did to deserve his undeniable love.

I hugged Jeff as we stood in the entryway. Carter was

waiting for him in the truck. "Please let your brother take care of you."

"I don't need a babysitter, Princess. I can take care of myself."

"Whatever. Enjoy your boys' weekend then. I'll have a girls' night out."

Jeff ran a hand over his scruffy face. He hadn't shaved in a week. He looked as messed up on the outside as he did on the inside. His navy shirt was wrinkled, and his jeans, which hung low on his hips since he'd lost a lot of weight, were ripped and stained with paint and mechanic oil.

"I love you," I said, the words burning the tip of my tongue as they exited my mouth. My Jeff made an appearance. Something glinted in his eyes. I blinked, unsure if I imagined the whole thing. No. It was there. A little glow brightening up his darkness.

My heart filled with sprinkles of hope.

Maybe we'd get through this.

Not today.

But one day.

Jeff cradled my cheeks. "I love you so much, Dah. I'll get better. I promise. Don't lose faith in me." I offered him a tight-lipped smile because that was all I could muster right now. "Say something. I know I've hurt you. More than enough times—This is hard. So freaking hard. I'll start working again. It would do me some good to see other people. I'll call Peter at the garage. You'll see. It's you and me, Princess."

I kissed him. I didn't know what to say. For a second, I wanted to believe him. To believe he'd get the help he needed. But how many times did we have the same conversation in the last few months? And each time, it ended up being just words thrown around to make me feel better. To infuse a false sense of hope in me.

Jeff hooked his hand around my neck.

When his tongue met mine, I dissolved in his arms. I placed a palm over his chest and let his heartbeat do the talking.

Jeff's hands traveled all over me. Heat pooled between my legs. How could his touch alone be powerful enough to ignite my body? To make me forget we were fighting seconds ago? A blazing fire raged inside me. My hand lowered and grabbed his erection over the fabric of his pants.

"Princess, I want you. Here and now. Please send my brother away. We need this. You and me."

I closed my eyes. Sex couldn't solve all our problems, but it was the only way we could connect. And nowadays, our bodies were better at communicating our feelings for each other than our words. Words hurt. Love made us forget about everything keeping us apart. It patched—for a few hours—the giant rift between us.

I fished my phone from the back pocket of my black denims.

Cart. I'll drive Jeff myself. Don't worry, we're ok.

I didn't wait for him to reply. I threw my phone on the black iron console by the front door.

"Just fuck me, already."

Jeff's irises blackened. Some sort of animal grunt left his mouth.

He scooped me over his shoulder and put me on my feet when we reached the couch. With jerky and clumsy movements, we undressed each other. Jeff's stubble left red marks on my sensitive skin. His mouth attacked mine. Hard. Soft. With hunger. With pleasure. With pain.

I moaned, unable to keep all the sounds bubbling down my throat clamped in.

Jeff slumped on the couch, bringing me with him. He shifted position, his head now in the opposite direction of mine, and lowered himself until his mouth collapsed with my throbbing center. My fingernails dug into the flesh of his abs as his tongue laved me with wide strokes, stealing my ability to speak.

My body, full of need, shook when his teeth toyed with my bundle of nerves.

I yelped.

Jeff inserted one finger inside me, his mouth still feasting on me.

I leaned forward and grabbed his thick length.

My mouth watered.

My tongue swirled around the tip of his cock, and Jeff's hips buckled from the couch.

My hand worked him as I alternated between sucking and licking him.

My boyfriend entered a second finger inside my walls, and my body tingled. All my senses heightened, and I came undone on his tongue, becoming hot mush under his touch.

Once I caught my breath, Jeff flipped me around until my back rested on the pile of pillows.

He thrust into me, his eyes glued to mine.

An entire movie passed in his irises.

His hands molded my breasts to fit them, pushing them up as he kissed them.

His tongue circled my nipples, sucking and licking my flesh.

A high-pitched cry left my mouth.

Jeff's hands clutched my hipbones, and he pounded

into me. My body hummed. My head turned. My heart started beating again.

There were so many things I wanted to tell this man. But I had no idea how to reach him with my words.

I squirmed underneath him, barely able to keep my eyes open, the waves of pleasure rippling through me.

Jeff groaned and slid out of me. He fisted his cock and stroked himself a few times until his hot and thick cum covered my belly.

With his finger, he traced a heart on my naked flesh with his cream, branding me. A glint flashed in his eyes.

"I changed my mind. I'll go on tour with you. I need you," he said in a rough voice.

I shook my head and sighed. "No. You're not coming. We need some time apart. To heal."

His face reddened, and a cloud of pain filled his eyes.

"Are you breaking up with me?"

"No. But we can't do this anymore. We fight all the time, and then we fuck like animals as if it could fix everything."

"We're good at this," Jeff said, motioning his hand between our naked bodies.

"Yes. But it's not enough. We need to be good again at being together outside the bedroom. Sex doesn't solve anything. You'll join me when you deal with whatever shit you need to deal with."

My boyfriend's body stiffened. The gleam in his eyes vanished.

My heart ached.

My throat clenched, and air barely made it to my brain, leaving me dizzy.

Jeff's chest rose. His throat bobbed. With a deep inhale, he closed his eyes.

"Is that an ultimatum?"

He exhaled and stared at me with so much intensity that my body quaked.

"It's for you to figure out." I rolled my lips over my teeth, forcing myself to shut up before saying everything that was on my mind.

Jeff looked away and breathed in before rising to his feet. "Fine. We'll do as you say. Don't bother driving me to Carter's, I'll walk."

He got dressed and left without another glance my way, slamming the door behind him. Leaving a hole, the size of Texas, in my soul.

Did I just destroy what was left of our relationship?

My heart fractured.

Pieces fell to the ground.

I was too tired to pick them up.

Instead, I buried my face in my hands and cried.

All the tears I had locked deep inside me for the last year.

I emptied the whole freaking well.

And then I emptied a second one.

13

DAHLIA

Seven months later

The vibration of my phone woke me up from a deep slumber. With the back of my hand, I wiped the drool that had pooled and dried at the corner of my lips. It took me a minute to remember I wasn't in my hotel suite. I tried to make out everything that happened last night.

Another piece of my heart had broken after Jeff and I argued over the phone, and I hung up on him. Even from thousands of miles apart, things were still strained between us. Most of the time. The powerlessness I felt, not knowing what to do to fix my relationship, and the sadness on knowing the one man I'd ever loved was slipping through my fingers, had turned my heart into a dark pit. We argued about everything and anything. Last night it was about not coming home on my five days break.

Our second world tour had been tiring, and I needed a few days to myself.

To recharge my batteries.

To reassess everything going on in my life.

We had a little more than a month left before the end of our tour, and the thought of going back home—for a year—got me angsty.

Since that day we promised each other that nothing would come between us, Jeff and I had changed. So damn much. The once selfless and sweet man I used to know had turned into a bitter and angry version of himself. And the worst was that he still refused to talk about any of it. PTSD was a bitch, and I had no idea how to deal with it. And love wasn't enough to patch every hole in someone's heart or sew the broken pieces back together. I'd learned that the hard way.

My man got lost. Somewhere in the Middle East. And never came back.

The breath of the man lying next to me eased my troubled thoughts for a moment—the ones stabbing my heart to a slow death. I eyed the butt-naked silhouette, covered in only a white sheet, in the semi-darkened room. Sleeping on his front, with his head turned to the side, and his strong and defined arms tucked under the pillow.

His dark, wavy hair fell over his eyes; his sleepy face was the definition of peace. A tightness grew in my chest. What did I do? I shouldn't have come here last night. This was bad. How could I have let all my guards down? When did I become so selfish?

Deep down, I knew why. I needed to feel loved. And wanted. And there was only one place I knew I would find it.

In the morning light, guilt clawed at the walls of my heart. I rubbed a hand over my face and tried to swallow the boulder down my throat.

Tears prickled the back of my eyes. *What did I do?*

My phone vibrated again, reminding me I hadn't checked it yet.

One missed call. And one text message.

**Jeff: Princess, please call me. I'm sorry.
Forgive me. I love you.**

My lungs collapsed. Ice replaced the warm blood in my veins.

I gasped.

Tears welled up in my eyes.

I rested my face in my hands.

Without a sound and choking on my sobs, I gathered my clothes that were spread all over the room. The scent of cedarwood and pine filled my nostrils. The scent that had always calmed me down. That had been mine.

For a night.

I eyed the full lips of the sleeping man. With my fore-finger, I traced my own, remembering how they felt on mine. How they tasted.

With shaky hands, I fumbled to clasp my bra. On wobbly legs, I put my panties and jeans on. Next, I pulled my sweater over my head. My eyes lingered on the man's lips. Again. I looked at him one last time before leaving him behind, still naked and asleep. I burned the picture of him into my brain. Flashes of last night passed before my eyes. My heart lurched in my throat.

Like a coward, I ran away, stealing a large chunk of his heart.

Would he ever forgive me?

And would I ever forgive myself?

I dried my tears with the back of my hands. I inhaled, the air hot as scorching fire as it reached my lungs. My hands strangled the doorknob as I opened the door. My own heart was broken into so many pieces, I feared a few would drop to the floor, leaving a trail of blood behind, as I retreated to my suite.

I tiptoed in the dimly lit hallway; the rest of the world had not woken up yet. Once in the safety of my room, the door locked behind me, I picked up my phone.

"Hi, it's me. You called?"

"I'm here. At the airport. I need to see you. To be with you. Can I come over?"

My heart sank in the deep end of my chest. I massaged my temples, my thoughts racing. What did I do? Why did I screw everything up? My hand curled around the column of my throat. The walls closed around me. Could Jeff hear the distress in my voice? The pain? The guilt?

"We're staying at the S Hotel downtown." Every word I spoke felt like acid. "I'll call the front desk, so they'll let you come up once you get here." I tried to infuse happiness into my voice, but all my emotions formed a tight ball down my throat, making every breath a challenge. "I've missed you too." Did I, though? Yes. I missed my Jeff. The version of him I loved. The man I knew he was underneath all this pain.

"I'm sorry for everything. Please wait for me. We need to talk."

We hung up, and I turned the shower on and called the front desk. The curtain of hot water from the rain showerhead hanging from the ceiling created a wall around me. It kept me safe from the train wreck my life had become. For a minute, at least. Soon it wasn't enough anymore. I needed to wash last night off me.

Every touch.

Every feeling.

Every scent.

Every kiss.

With a washcloth, I rubbed my skin until it turned red. With my fingertips, I scrubbed my scalp, removing all memories of the hands that didn't belong to Jeff on me.

I felt dirty.

My stomach churned. Bile rose at the back of my throat.

Never in my life had I reached such a low point. When did I become a cheater? When did I stop fighting for what was mine? When did I turn into this version of me?

Last night, it all seemed so simple. Just a man and a woman loving each other. Needing each other's comfort to get through the night. No questions asked. No promises made. It just felt right. Like it was meant to be.

In the morning light, it didn't seem so black or white anymore.

With a white towel wrapped around me, I brushed my teeth, avoiding my reflection in the three-panel mirror, removing the taste of the man's lips on mine.

Once satisfied, I dressed in a pair of yoga pants and a dark-purple knitted sweater.

The soft knock on the door startled me.

I sucked in a breath, ragged and shallow, and with a straight back, I opened the door.

Jeff stared at me from the other side of the threshold, with blood-shot eyes, chapped and swollen lips, and an unruly scrub covering his jaw, his hair untamed and long.

We hadn't seen each other in four months.

The last time was when we played in Canada and his brother invited him to join us for a few days. Things had been strained even then. We didn't even share a room that weekend. Jeff bunked with Carter.

During his stay, we had sex. Many times. But other than those times, we failed to connect, the tension so high between us, it affected the band. Stud had pulled me to the side one night, asking me to deal with my shit. Yeah, that bad.

Right now, in the hotel hallway, Jeff looked nothing like the man I used to know. And yet, a glint in his eyes reminded me he was still in there as he gave me a slow once-over.

The sight of him standing there, his shoulders rolled forward, his hands stuffed in his pockets, a bag at his feet, looking like a lost child, tugged at all my heartstrings.

I forgot everything about my night of shame.

Nothing mattered more than this man. The one who crossed half the world in a night to be with me. The one I had always loved more than life itself. The one I could never get enough of. My heart woke up. It started beating again.

God, I've missed him.

With one quick intake of air, I ran into his arms. When they closed around me, shielding me from the world, all the broken pieces of my heart fused back together.

Jeff lifted me, and I wound my legs around his waist.

"I'm so sorry, Princess. I love you. I don't want to fight anymore. The last few months have been hell. I can't live without you. You're my heart. My soul. You own every bit of me. Will you ever be able to forgive me?"

His lips crashed on mine, careful at first, and then hungry and needy.

A turmoil of renewed passion filled me.

I traced the outline of his face with my hands, memorizing the shape of his lips, the high cheekbones, the straight nose under the pads of my thumbs.

"I can't believe you're here." My voice broke. "That you came back to me," I said between sobs. Jeff nodded, keeping his gaze to the floor.

"Always."

Tears clouded my vision. "I can't fight with you anymore. I'm not strong enough. But I'm not ready to let you go. You own every piece of me too." I sniffled. Jeff's arms tightened around me. "How long are you staying?"

"Forever, Princess. I'm never letting you go again. I'm staying for the rest of the tour or as long as you'll have me. I'm not going back home if you're not by my side. I can't live when you're not there. I can't sleep when you're mad at me. I never want to put tears in your eyes ever again. I love you too damn much. Don't lose hope in me. In us. We'll be good. I promise. It's you and me."

I anchored myself to this man. My man. The one owning me. Heart and soul.

"What about the grief, the nightmares, the anger?"

I pulled back so we could look at each other. I needed to look him in the eyes.

"I've been seeing someone. A shrink. It's helping. It'll get better. Yesterday's fight pushed me over the edge. But it also made me realize how awful I've been to you since I came back. You did nothing but love me. And all I did was push you away. Or let my anger rule me. I can't live like this anymore. I'll get all the help I need. Just don't walk out on us."

Jeff's fingers caressed my face. His lips kissed my tears away and replaced them with hope. Little seeds that suggested we could get through this. Together.

"You look like shit." For the first time in a long, long while, Jeff's lips curled into a ghost of a smile. "Go take a shower. Since I have the day off, we'll sleep in." I tugged at his hand and pulled him into the room.

I dried off my wet cheeks with the sleeve of my sweater.

"I'm sorry, Dahlia. I'm sorry for everything I put you through. This won't happen again—"

With my fingers, I wiped off his tears. "It's okay. Shhh. Don't cry. It's okay. I love you. We'll be okay. It's you and me, remember?"

Before joining Jeff in the shower, I called Carter.

"Hey," he answered, his voice rough from sleep. No doubt I just woke him up.

I kept my voice low, not wanting Jeff to eavesdrop on my conversation. "Hey, Carter. Jeff's here."

All traces of sleep vanished from his voice. "You're kidding, right?"

"I wish. He called earlier to let me know he was on his way. He wanted to surprise us. Please don't say a word to him. It'll break his heart. Please, Carter."

I could imagine him scratching his forehead, like he always did when he was nervous. "I won't." He cleared his throat. My hair raised on end all over my body. I swallowed hard. "When is he leaving? We need to—we need to talk."

I said nothing for a few seconds. "He's not. He's staying for the rest of the tour. Carter, I need to go. We'll talk later." And I hung up—not ready to face the mess my life had become lately—and joined Jeff in the shower, letting the water wash all my sins away. Again.

The next morning, I woke up to my man kissing my jaw, his hard length pressed between my thighs. My body vibrated underneath his. My throat closed up. Tears burned the back of my eyes, and a tightness coiled around my heart. "Good morning, Princess." His gruff voice sent shivers through me.

When he leaned closer to kiss me, I turned my head to the side.

I blinked away the wall of tears messing with my vision.

Jeff pulled back and kneeled beside me. His hands

framed my face, and he brushed the river across my cheeks away.

"I'm sorry. What was I thinking? It's too soon. I've just missed you so much—" His voice cracked. "I don't want us to be this way, Dahlia. I'm tired of the ice walls between us. I want to let you in. I'm ready." My silent tears turned into wracking sobs. "Don't cry, Princess. I'm right here. I won't leave you ever again. You're the most important person in my life."

Jeff lay behind me and wrapped his arms around my shuddering body, pulling me close to his heart. Where I belonged. He kissed the back of my head and my bare shoulder.

"I love you," I whispered with a croaky voice. "We'll be okay. I want us to be okay."

"We're stronger than this."

The heaviness of my eyelids won the battle, and feeling each thump of Jeff's heart behind my shoulder blades, I dozed off, whispers of hope making their way to my bruised heart.

The next day, Jeff and I stayed in our hotel suite, trying to put back together all the torn pieces of our hearts. We had months to make up for. Dressed in white bathrobes, we ordered room service for breakfast, lunch, and dinner.

"I don't remember the last time we spent a day doing nothing but watching TV," Jeff said as my head rested in his lap, and he brushed strands of my copper hair away from my face. "But somehow it feels right. Maybe we should move in here and never get out."

I chuckled. "I'm sure we'd both be fat by the end of the month. It's not normal eating that much ice cream and chocolate mousse in just a day."

"I'd love you no matter what, Princess. If you want us

to be fat together, just say the word. I'm so gone for you, and at this point, I'll do whatever you ask of me."

"Don't be silly. What have you done to Jeff? The guy who lifted weights before going to bed when he was eighteen years old?"

My man untied his terry cloth bathrobe and with a wink, flashed me his chest muscles. "You're talking about these, Princess? They're still there. You've missed them?"

"You know I did. But I'd like you even without your washboard." I flipped on my other side and nuzzled his stomach.

Jeff entangled his fingers in my hair. "I've missed you. All of you."

"Why are you here?"

"Because I needed to see you. I already told you that —" I placed a finger over his lips.

"I want the ugly truth."

He cocked his head to the side, inhaled, and brought his gaze back on me.

"The last time we fought, you hung up on me. At first, I was upset with you. But then I did a reality check and didn't like what I saw. I'd become a cliché. I was watching a stupid show on TV, drinking beer as if it was water, dressed in dirty sweatpants and a white wifebeater. I don't want to be a stupid joke. I'm afraid I'll lose you if I keep going down the rabbit hole. This isn't a life. I'm better than this. Than my demons. I'm not back to being myself quite yet, but now for the first time in a long time, I'm willing to get the help I need and be the man you deserve. I'm on new meds, and they're helping with the anxiety."

I swallowed hard. With my eyes closed, I sucked in a jagged breath.

"Thanks for telling me all this."

Jeff scooted on the sofa and pulled me to him. "Come

here, Princess. I want to hold you till the morning." I sank my body in his, and Jeff covered us with the white Sherpa blanket I brought from the bedroom earlier. "Good night. I love you."

My eyelids grew heavy. The last two days had been a roller coaster of emotions. "I love you. Don't ever let me go," I said, fighting a yawn.

"Never."

———

The next morning, I woke up with a stiff neck. Did we spend the entire night on the sofa? I scanned the room, the morning sunlight casting a golden glow in the living room through the floor-to-ceiling panoramic windows. A smile tugged at my lips. Jeff tightened his grip around my waist. Everything seemed brighter this morning. Flutters danced in my belly. Something I hadn't felt in a long while.

Jeff squirmed beside me but didn't wake up. He was so handsome and looked so peaceful.

As if it was the first time, I grazed my lips over his. Once. Twice.

I filled my lungs with oxygen.

Jeff's hand lowered to my ass, and he grabbed a handful of one cheek.

The fuzzy feelings in my belly returned.

"Please love me," I said, my voice low. "I need to feel every inch of you in and on me."

Jeff raised his head, and his eyes met mine. Desire, need, and fear swam in his dark irises. "You sure?"

I nodded. "Yeah." A lone tear rolled down my cheek, and I brushed it away. "I need you. All of you."

Jeff's large and muscular hand locked behind my head and he crashed his lips on mine.

With jerky movements, we removed each other's bathrobes, our mouths glued together. Heat filled my lower belly. An ache settled between my thighs. My hands lingered on Jeff's warm chest. With my finger, I traced a line along his happy trail. His cock bulged in his black boxer briefs, and my mouth watered at the sight of him, all thick and hard for me.

Lust dripped from Jeff's eyes, and wetness pooled between my legs.

With a quick intake of breath, I pushed the guilt of my shameful night away, wanting to lose myself in the man I loved until we both forgot who we were. Jeff's thumbs hooked into the waistband of my white cotton panties and pulled them down my legs. My eyes sprang open when his warm breath met the apex of my thighs. *God, I've missed him. I've missed this.* Jeff knew my body like a roadmap leading to his home. And Jeff was my home. As I was his. My body shuddered as my man's lips and tongue circled my clit. He feasted on me like I was his favorite snack. He fucked me with his tongue until my body buckled off the bed. Until I lost all sense of time and space. Until I came with such force that I fisted his hair, and he yelped.

For a minute, Jeff hovered over me, his eyes burning holes into my skin. Panting, his face glossy from the way he cherished my pussy. He looked so damn hot.

With my finger, I motioned him to come closer.

Once we faced each other, I rose to my knees, and with both hands splayed on Jeff's shoulders, I pushed him backward. I combed the wild strands of his hair away from his forehead. I wanted to see him. All of him. His eyes darkened. His lips straightened. He clutched my hips, and we studied each other for a long minute. My nipples stiffened. My entire body tingled from the contact of our naked flesh. Jeff's chest rose and fell.

"You're so beautiful, Princess." I leaned forward to kiss him. As if it was the first time. And the last. With restraint. Without control. And with everything I possessed. Jeff deepened the kiss. "Ride me, baby. I want to watch you."

A smug grin brightened his face. There was no more trace of the sadness that had painted his features for the last two days.

As his hands traveled down my body, I untangled myself from his grip and turned around, straddling my man reverse-cowgirl style. Instead of engulfing his thick cock inside me, I sat on his chest and leaned forward until my tongue teased his tip. Jeff's length pulsed between my lips. He cursed under his breath. With every swirl of my tongue, a loud, guttural groan left his mouth. Each one increasing the ache between my legs.

Jeff didn't even have to touch me to turn me into molten clay. Into a blaze.

While I pumped him in long strokes and sucked him to oblivion, Jeff's thumb found my wet center and dove in. He slid his ass down a little on the sofa, and with both hands, he lifted my ass until his mouth could lick all the juices coming out of me in waves.

I lost my rhythm, my pleasure taking over.

His breathing quickened, tickling my flesh.

"Babe, turn over. I need to be inside you. Now. I won't last. We have too fucking long to make up for." Instead of facing Jeff, I stayed with my back to his front, and his dick speared into me. I wouldn't look him in the eyes—because I couldn't. Guilt was crippling me. I wasn't ready to let him see through me. One day we'd talk about this. Right now, we were both broken and needed each other's comfort. And each other's love.

Jeff's magnetism sucked me in. As if no time had passed since the last time we were together. He touched me, and I liquified. Then he molded me in his hands, my body craving the pleasure he always brought me.

I rode him until we were both sweaty and breathless. With his hands clutching my hips, he lifted his ass from the bed and rammed into me. Harder. Faster. Slower. Gentler. With care. With fierceness. With everything he could give me. Before we both came, I rose to my hands and knees, and with one hand tangled in my hair, Jeff pounded into me from behind, his other hand rubbing my hard-as-rock nipple between his thumb and forefinger.

I cried.

All the pain and pleasure, the guilt and shame inside me mixed together.

I steeled my back, and Jeff circled one arm around me, tugging me to him, my back to his hard chest. He pushed into me one last time, and we both crumpled on the sofa. Spent. And closer than we'd been in years.

———

Five weeks later

This couldn't be right. "It's a mistake; it's not real," I screamed at no one but me. "Life is just messing with you. It's your punishment for the stupid thing you did."

I dropped the white plastic stick on the floor of the hotel room. We were in Australia. For the closing show of our second world tour tomorrow night.

I gasped, trying to bring some air into my lungs.

Not working.

I slammed the door. It wasn't enough to ease my nerves.

The all-white walls of the giant bathroom closed in on me. I hated this immaculate decor. It reminded me of a funeral house. Where they put caskets behind thick stoned walls instead of in the ground. The bathtub was huge with large columns around it. If the goal was to give the impression we were in some sort of Mediterranean decor, they failed. It was one of the most prestigious hotels in Sydney. And yet, it looked ugly.

Another wave of nausea hit me. My mouth filled with that disgusting acidic taste. I pressed my hand over my belly, trying to ease everything inside me. I felt sick. And it didn't help I'd been throwing up all week.

Until now, I'd convinced myself I caught a stomach bug.

Now I knew different.

Just the thought of it made my insides churn.

Hot tears etched the delicate skin of my cheeks.

Everything went dark.

Curled in a ball on the shiny tiled white floor, I picked up the stick as I heard Jeff's voice, laced with fear and dipped in so much love.

This last month together had been good. Really good. We were becoming Jeff and Dahlia all over again.

His voice came closer. I heard him, but I couldn't talk, my tongue thick in my mouth. The back of my eyes burned from all the tears I shed. The soft knock on the door startled me.

"Hey, Dah, are you in here?" Carefully, Jeff squatted beside me. "Ohmygod, are you still sick? You should go see a doctor?"

I shook my head.

"Princess, don't be stubborn. You're pale. And weak. You're shaking. I'll call the reception, maybe they can send someone over."

I shook my head again, clutching his forearm.

"How long have you been in here?"

I shrugged. As if I had a clue. Jeff fished his phone from his back pocket.

"I was gone for less than two hours. Did you try to call me? Or Carter? You knew we were having lunch together."

I said nothing, a sob, sounding more like a shriek, breaking the fragile silence in the room.

"Princess, talk to me. Did I do that to you? I thought we were over this. I thought we were doing okay."

So much pain sliced through his words.

No way I'd let him blame himself.

"I'm not sick, Jeff. I'm pregnant—"

The words tasted awful on the tip of my tongue.

Once they were out, I couldn't take them back.

Jeff pulled my shoulders to help me sit on his lap.

"You're pregnant—" Was it a question or a statement? I didn't know.

"I am." That was all I could say. With the hem of my robe, the one with the high-end hotel logo on it—all white, like the rest of this ugly room—I wiped off my cheeks.

The flesh underneath my eyes was raw, like an open wound. Same as my heart.

"How? When? You're still on the pill?"

"Yes." I took a deep breath. "You know the thing I take for jet lag. It might have interfered with it. I don't know."

"Dahlia, why are you crying? It's good news. It's terrific news. I'm gonna be a father. A daddy. Who would've thought? You'll be an amazing mother. We're going to be a family. You and me." His hand found my stomach and rested there. "And this tiny baby. I promise you, here and now, I'll be the best father in the entire world." I didn't doubt that. But was the baby even Jeff's?

A few weeks ago, I messed up.

And now life was making me pay for my mistake.

In the most ironic way.

A baby was growing inside me, and I had no idea who the father was.

Big fucking joke.

In my life, I'd always been the nice and sweet child, the responsible and mature teenager, the focused and smart adult. And now this. I'd made one mistake. One stupid—well, at the time it didn't feel stupid—mistake and I'd have to live with that bad decision hanging over my head for the rest of my life.

I knew I needed to come clean.

But right now, as twinkles danced in Jeff's dark irises and he held me as if I were made of gold and diamonds, I couldn't risk breaking his heart.

All the clouds that had been fogging his eyes for so long had vanished. All gone.

My Jeff was back. Every last piece of him.

I could tell.

And a small smile broke free on my face. I'd missed him so much. Never would I have thought he'd come back to me. And there he was, proving me all wrong.

One day I'd tell him.

But not today.

14

JEFFREY

I wanted to scream for the universe to hear. I was going to be a daddy. The word sounded foreign coming out of my mouth. But I'd seen the stick. Two pink lines. There was no doubt. I'd be a father. Soon. The part of my heart that got lost in the desert came back. The missing parts I'd been looking for, for quite some time, and those I thought I'd never get back. A daddy. Could I ever get used to this word?

"Please don't tell the guys before we're done with the show tomorrow," Dahlia asked me. "And I want to be the one telling Carter."

"Are you sure you don't want us to tell him together?"

Dahlia shook her head. "No. Please. Let me do this."

I slumped my shoulders. "Fine. But I need to do something, and it can't wait. Let's get you cleaned up and dressed."

"Or we can stay here. Locked up in this awful bathroom."

I jumped to my feet. "Sorry. Can't do this. I want to go now. It can't wait."

A spark of curiosity appeared in Dahlia's eyes, chasing some of her tears away.

Why was Dahlia so torn up about being pregnant? After everything we'd been through in the last two years, this was the best news we could ever have. It was life's way of fitting all the broken parts of our lives back together.

That was why, right now, I knew the thought filling my head couldn't wait. In the last few months, I promised myself that if Dahlia and I were strong enough to patch things up between us, I would do this. It wasn't a spur-of-the-moment decision. I'd been thinking about it since I was seventeen years old and madly in love with my brother's best friend. Back when nobody knew about my infatuation for the copper-haired girl with the voice of an angel.

Back then I dated Vanessa, forcing myself to forget about Dahlia. But whatever I did or however much I tried, it never worked. Dahlia crept under my skin when I wasn't even ten years old and never left.

Dressed in an emerald-green wrap dress, wearing brown cowboy boots, her hair tied in a thick braid, my girl was a vision. My vision. My dick twitched at the sight of her. How did I ever push her away? Would I be able to forgive myself? I broke her heart after I promised I'd never do it.

I swallowed all the emotions rising up my throat. If I let these out, we would both drown in them. There were just too many of them bottled up inside me.

Even in my darkest hours, Dahlia was the light leading me back home. My star to follow. My aim. My goal.

"You look absolutely amazing," I told her as she snaked her arms around me. I leaned forward to claim her mouth. The mouth that could rob me of all self-control, and also ignite my entire being.

"Where are you taking me?"

"It's a surprise. First, we'll go somewhere, then we'll have dinner. With fake champagne and all your favorite food. I want to spoil you."

Dahlia's eyes glazed.

"I hope I'll be able to keep it all in."

"We'll only eat ice cream if that's what you crave. Anything for you."

Billy, one of the Band's security guys, shadowed us. My girlfriend, my brother, and Stud were now rich and famous. Everybody wanted a piece of them. They had crazy fans following them around the globe. Carter had a lineup of groupies, begging to be fucked by him. As if his dick were a stick made of gold that would make them orgasm ten times stronger. Who cared, really? I just hoped my brother used his head better than he used his golden dick.

Stud forwent the idea of one-nighters. After their first world tour, he started dating his personal assistant, Belinda. She followed him on the road all the time. They never had to deal with the long-distance relationship Dahlia and I had to go through.

"Are you ready, Princess?"

Dahlia smiled my way, her moss-green eyes sucking me in. The same way they'd been drawing me in for the twenty years I'd known her.

I leaned over until our lips collided. "Everything will be okay. I love you. Don't worry about a thing. I'm here, and I'm not going anywhere ever again."

Earlier, I took Billy to the side and explained my plan. He drove us to King Street after making a phone call, assuring Dahlia and me some privacy and access through the back door, where nobody would see us going in.

That was what my girl's life had become nowadays. Everywhere we went, people recognized her.

Dahlia locked her arm through mine as we exited the black-tinted car. "Where are we?" From the alley, the brownstone building didn't give a clue what it hid inside its walls. Billy knocked on the door, and a man in his fifties with long blond locks let us in.

He smiled at Dahlia and shook my hand.

"Follow me, Mr. Hills."

I laced my fingers through my girl's, and we entered a small room. A display of engagement rings, each more sparkly than the next, filled two rectangular tables.

"I'll let you take a look and be right back in a few minutes to answer any questions you might have."

Dahlia's eyes widened, and I heard her quick intake of air.

"Jeff—What—This is—" I dropped on one knee. She gasped, bringing both her hands over her mouth.

"Dahlia Ellis, I've loved you since I was ten years old. And I'll love you forever. I'm sorry I've been such a mess in the last two years. But no matter how angry I was at the world, nothing I've felt for you has ever changed. You were with me when I was battling for our country, here in my heart. You're with me even when you're on the other side of the world, chasing your dreams. You're everything I want in this life. You and our baby. Don't cry, Princess." I jumped to my feet to dry her tears. "We're in this together. No matter what. I want you to be my wife. Now and forever. In my heart, I've been married to you since the day you walked on that stage in your red dress and flying pigtails. You own my heart and my soul with your smile, your voice, your kindness, and your strength. You even sneaked out of your parents' house at seventeen to be with me. When I bought the house, I knew I'd want to live there with you. Build a family with you and then move because we wouldn't have enough rooms to fit all our children.

"You are my dream. My past. My present. My future. I know we didn't plan for this baby, but we'll be fine. We'll be great. Because I love you, and I know how much you love me. You show me every time you look at me, smile at me, or even fight with me. Because you care. You care so much. It's you and me. Forever. Until we're all gray and old." I leaned forward to kiss the tears on her cheeks. "Princess, will you marry me?"

Dahlia said nothing. She looked at me from under her curtain of tears. My pulse throbbed. I squeezed her hands in mine. Why wasn't she saying anything? A lump built in my throat. Knots grew in my stomach.

"Princess—?"

She jumped into my arms, her legs around my middle, her green dress bulking around her waist. Without a word, she nodded, a grin plastered on her beautiful face.

"I'll marry you any day, Jeff. I love you so damn much. You're sure you're ready for all this?"

"I'll marry you tomorrow if you let me."

"You know our parents will kill us, right? They'll think we're too young to commit."

"I don't care. All I want is you. Everybody else can go to hell."

Dahlia chose a trio of diamonds set on a platinum band. All princess-y.

Seated beside her at the semicircle table of the restaurant I chose for tonight, I stared at my *fiancée*'s ringless finger and sighed.

Dahlia leaned into my arms and pressed my chest with one hand, the other stroking me over the fabric of my pants under the table, an innocent smile pasted on her face, her red-painted lips enticing. "Don't worry, we'll pick it up in two days. I'm still your *fiancée*," she said with a wink. We were celebrating our engagement, enjoying sparkling apple cider in crystal glasses, instead of expensive champagne. "The ring is just a bonus. But it doesn't change the fact that we're getting married."

I sighed, hating the idea we had to wait two days for it to be resized.

"You know, I'll never be able to wait. I want to marry you today. Once back home, we'll set everything up. I've been waiting long enough already to call you my wife."

"We have a couple of shows scheduled before our break."

"We'll work around your schedule, Princess. And once the baby is born, we'll take the longest honeymoon known to mankind."

Dahlia removed her hands from my body and clamped them between her thighs. All traces of playfulness vanished from her features.

"Jeff, I've been thinking—I want to quit the band." She spoke the words as if they bore no weight. I choked on my alcohol-free drink.

"You what?"

She shrugged. "With the baby and everything, it's the right thing to do. I want to pursue other dreams. Carter is the star. I was just helping him get there. Now he can shine on his own."

I blinked. Once the wave of shock subsided, I asked, "And what does Carter think about all this?"

Dahlia lowered her gaze.

My brother didn't know. It would destroy him.

Dahlia was his entire world too.

"He doesn't know it. I wanted to run it by you first.

Please don't tell him just yet. I'll talk to him tomorrow night. After the show. I'll clear the air up. About everything."

She offered me a shy smile, and it soothed some of my angst.

"You're sure about this? I don't want you to make any rushed decisions. You have a few months off. Perhaps you should take some time to think it over."

"Jeff, I won't change my mind. I want us. We've put ourselves on the back burner for too long. I hate living in hotel suites and having people chase me in the streets. Sure, I love music, but this life isn't for me. I'll choose quiet family and fun with you over any fame. I'm telling you; I'll be happier this way."

I relaxed my shoulders. Drunk on Dahlia's eyes, I offered her a crooked smile.

"That honeymoon thing just got more interesting, Princess."

I winked at her, and her hands traveled back to my crotch. Her grip on me tightened.

"If you don't stop, we'll never make it through dinner. Are the pregnancy hormones supposed to make you hornier from the start?"

Dahlia's smile doubled its size. "It's not the hormones. It's you. You're making me horny."

I could die right now, and I'd die a lucky man.

———

The bottle of whiskey crashed on the wall inches from my head. "What the actual fuck, little bro?" I asked as I took in the fury in Carter's glazed eyes. "Have you lost your mind?"

Carter pinned me against the wall with his stare in a

way he'd never done before. His hands clenched and unclenched at his sides; his knuckles turned white. The pulse in his neck, visible from where I stood, picked up, and his eyes became the laser beams shredding me to pieces.

Darkness swirled around him as his demons took over and buried everything good in him into a hollow pit.

"Just get the fuck out," he barked, the air in the room getting heavier by the second.

"Man, we're supposed to be boarding the plane right now. Everyone's worried about you. We need to go." I took a skittish step in his direction, my hands raised in surrender. I kept my tone low and steady. "Never thought the idea of getting a three-month break after traveling the world for the last eight months would do that to you."

My attempt at a joke backfired.

"Don't talk about what you don't know, big bro. For everyone's sake, keep your stupid mouth shut."

And then it hit me. Damn it. I cringed. Why didn't I think about it first?

I braced myself, firmed my back, and cleared my throat. "Did Dahlia talk to you last night?"

"You bet she did. She—"

The madness in my brother's eyes splashed the entire hotel suite. Red-hot splatters made of blood. Right from his heart.

I stepped forward, but he cocked his head to the side, his eyes shut. I waited. One, two, three, ten minutes. When Carter's eyes opened and drifted back to me, they were bloodshot and glossy. His throat worked. With the heels of his hands over his face, he hid his tears from me.

"I—I'm sorry. For everything." I swallowed the rock lodged in my throat. "I know you love her. That you've always loved her." I fought my own tears back and raked my hands through my hair. "But I feel for her too. Even when we were just kids. It has always been her, Cart. No matter how hard I tried to stay away, she was pulling me in, without even knowing it. I'm so sorry—"

Carter snorted, his hands still covering his pain-tinged face.

When he moved his hands down, I stopped breathing. We faced each other, and for the first time in my life, a rift separated us. An endless black hole ready to swallow us both in. Carter and I stood on opposite sides of the chasm, and I had no idea how to reach out to him. How to save him from so much suffering. We fought about Dahlia before, but this time was different. She was pregnant with my child. We were getting married. Carter could never have her. And I felt for him. Bad.

He cleared his throat. "I—" But the words died on his tongue. He collapsed on the floor, his legs folded, and his head buried between his knees. My heart broke as I witnessed his distress. My baby brother had always been the strong one. The fun one. The happy one. The smart one. My heart hurt because right now, I was the reason he was in agony. Me. His older brother—the one who was supposed to watch over him, to protect him—and I failed him. He trusted me, and I tore his heart apart by falling for his best friend. And she was also quitting the band—their band—to spend more time with me.

My chest split in two.

Wiping my tears in the crook of my elbow, I squatted down beside my brother and pulled him into my arms.

Sobs rocked his body.

"I'm sorry. Just know I never planned to break your heart. I'll give you your space. To heal. And I hope one day you'll forgive me. And find your soulmate too. The one you're supposed to be with."

We stayed like this for a very long time. Our hearts bleeding for the same copper-haired girl we'd both loved our entire life.

Dahlia could've had Carter all along, but she chose me. Why did it feel so wrong right now? I closed my eyes, tears streaming down my face. "I love you, Carter." A veil of black-inked darkness descended upon us, but thoughts of the baby jolted my heart back to life. I had to think about my child. Make it my priority. My lips curled up at the realization that Dahlia and I would become a family. I huffed. It all seemed surreal.

Carter's hotel suite door opened, and my girl, my *fiancée*, the mother of my unborn child, slipped in, worry flooding her moss-green eyes. After she scanned the room —broken furniture, a shattered whiskey bottle, a hole in the wall—her gaze landed on Carter and me, still entangled on the floor. When our eyes met, the hurt I saw in hers broke another chunk of my heart. Her lips quivered. Tears streamed down her cheeks.

Dahlia neared us, and I bet if I looked close enough, I would see her heart beating through her shirt, bleeding the same color as Carter's and mine.

The air in the room thickened.

All these years, lost in our love, we'd never realized how much we'd been hurting the only other person who mattered the most to both of us.

Dahlia kneeled before us. Her perfume, some floral scent she'd been wearing since she was fifteen, swirled around the room and killed some of the tension.

She took a quick intake of air. Jolts of pain fired through me.

"Let me do this," she said, her voice soft, like a lullaby soothing the demon hovering over us. "Let me take care of him, Jeff. Please." She begged me with her eyes as more tears soaked her angel face. Dahlia placed her hands on Carter's, and his shoulders relaxed a little at her touch. "Cart, it's me. Let me in." Without lifting his head, Carter nodded. As if she'd done it a million times before, Dahlia unfolded his arms and squeezed herself in between them. They both rested their foreheads against each other. Something powerful existed between them. It always had. Something I'd never be a part of. Something I'd never understand, no matter how hard I tried.

Feeling like an outsider, privy to a scene I wasn't a part of—or welcomed into—I rose to my feet. "I'll take his stuff to the car. Just meet us when you're ready." My girl nodded, her focus on my brother never faltering.

"I've got you," I heard her whisper as I shut the door behind me, a tightness growing in my chest.

Outside the suite, I met Carter's chief of security, standing by his door, ready to escort him downstairs. "Give them some time," I said, my voice laced with emotions, my head hanging low.

The plane ride back to Tennessee took forever. Carter slept almost the entire time. Dahlia sat beside me—sometimes on my lap—but her mind was far away. Sadness clung to her like an invisible cape. This time, not even my love or my words cleared the fog thickening around her.

Exhausted, we made it home the next day. We hadn't been here together in months, and the ghosts from the last time we were here, fighting, still lingered in the air. Even the upcoming wedding and the baby on the way weren't enough to lighten up the tension.

Dahlia had dark bags under her eyes and an aura of defeat in her usual proud stance. She looked frail and broken. My heart cracked.

I dropped all our luggage in our bedroom and made

her a cup of tea. With our hands linked, we sat on the couch.

"Princess, talk to me. Something's happened, I can sense it. It's all over you. Hurt. And sadness." I held her hands in mine. "Please don't shut me out. I thought we were doing better. Do you regret saying yes?" Knots tied my stomach as the words escaped my mouth. Were the last few days just a dream? Something I made up in my mind? Dahlia twisted her engagement ring around between her fingers. A lone tear cascaded down her face. She wiped it away with her fingertips. But soon more joined in, and her face turned into a canvas of pain that burned down pieces of my heart. Dahlia lowered her head, her shoulders heaving from the sobs rocking through her.

"I slept with him." The words tumbled out of her mouth, breaking the gears of my heart. More sobs. "Once." Oxygen didn't reach my brain. I blinked. My vision blurred. A hole opened below me, threatening to eat me alive.

It didn't make sense. I heard her wrong. With my fingers, I rubbed my ears. Shards of glass filled my veins.

"What?" Flames licked the lining of my throat as I spewed the word. The only word I could get out.

Dahlia sobbed, and all I wanted to do was to comfort her. To hold on to her. To hug her—all of her—and promise her we'd be okay. Instead, I stood there, frozen. How could we ever be okay again? My *fiancée* fucking slept with my brother.

My stomach leaped into my throat.

Instead of leaning over her, I leaned back and jumped to my feet, putting as much distance as possible between us.

Dahlia finally met my eyes. Hers were red, swollen, and full of regrets—or that's what they looked to me—and mine were—or I assumed they were—full of dark, flaming rage.

I unleashed my fury at her. I yelled. I punched the wall, making another dent in the drywall—man, it hurt. I tugged at the roots of my hair and cursed.

Pain poured out in waves from my crying girlfriend—or *fiancée*. Was she still even mine? The thought sent another wave of sickness up my throat.

On weak legs, I paced the living room like a lion who'd skipped a meal and about to attack anyone getting too close.

"No. No, no, no. I can't do this. I'm sorry. I can't stay here," I yelled.

With a deep inhale, I swallowed down my anger, grabbed my truck keys and a bottle of whiskey, and bolted for the door, almost ripping it from the hinges as I jerked it open.

Outside, the fresh air dissipated some of my misery away. My bleeding heart banged against my ribs. "I can't do this," I screamed. My hands shook. I took a long pull of the dark-golden liquor, welcoming the familiar sting down my throat. My life was a stupid joke. Everything I'd always taken for granted mattered no more. The two most important people in my life, the ones I'd give my life for without blinking an eye, had played me.

I raised the whiskey bottle to the sky, and with a mouthful of alcohol, I shouted, "Cheers to family and trust. All of you, go to hell—"

I brought the bottle back to my lips and downed half of it.

"Screw you all—"

My screams blended into sobs. My head swam into a booze bliss. A laugh, foreign and mimicking a growl, bubbled out. I zoomed in on the truck, keys still in my hand, my eyes out of focus. A brief spark of sanity made it through the fogginess of my brain. I was too intoxicated to drive. Before I numbed more brain cells, I spun on my heels and threw my keys as far as I could. They landed somewhere near the rosebush Dahlia planted when I first bought the house. Because she said it looked homier this way.

Big joke.

I looked around. Nothing around me felt like home anymore. Another wicked laugh rolled from my mouth. My eyes shot up, and I stared at the sky, gray and menacing. For a moment, I wished the rain would pour on me and drown my sorrows.

Hoping for a storm, and with a hand stuffed in my pocket and the other holding the bottle, I stumbled away, distancing myself from my life or everything I thought was mine. For two hours, maybe four—I didn't care—I waddled around, thoughts swirling chaotically in my head. I was mad at the world. At Dahlia. At Carter. And at myself. For a long while, I'd been awful to Dahlia. And I couldn't blame her for seeking some comfort away from me. But why did it have to be with my brother? My own blood? Irony. Karma was a nasty bitch. I was the one who begged Carter to look after her. He didn't need to look out for her that way. *Nice job, Jeff.* Damn it. I kicked the ground, a cloud of pebbles and dust soaring before me.

With one last gulp, I sucked the last drop of my whiskey and kept going, nursing the empty bottle like a newborn. I passed a local bar and hesitated to go in. The urge to enter the shady place and go on a killing spree passed through my mind. But I laughed it out. Yeah, like I was that guy. Killing somebody wouldn't resolve anything. I'd seen death. And it broke me. Never again.

I moved forward. I was so intoxicated I could barely lift

my feet from the ground. I looked around. Tall trees, dirty country roads. Where was I? I shrugged. Who cared? I wasn't missed anywhere. By anybody.

Miles later, I spotted a familiar fence. The entrance of Milwaukee Park. A shitload of memories flashed before my eyes, settling on the day I loitered there, gathering some courage to ask Dahlia to prom. It seemed like a lifetime away. So much had happened since that day. On a bench, my legs wide and my arms spread at my sides, I watched two guys about my age throwing a football on the green grassy patch. Hours passed. The gray sky darkened into the night. The rain never came. Some anger had left me. I breathed in. And out.

On weak legs, I resumed my walk. I passed my parents' house but didn't stop. Behind a bush, I took a leak, my bladder about to explode. As I zipped myself up, I hiccupped, and my stomach churned from the aftertaste of alcohol on my tongue.

When I made it back home, somehow calmer, I found Dahlia curled up in a ball on the couch, a pink fluffy blanket thrown over her body and her copper hair spread all over the pillow, looking like a halo around her head. With my back resting on the doorframe and my arms crossed over my chest, I stared at her. Her tears had carved trenches on her porcelain skin. She looked so young and vulnerable.

Why did I run away instead of talking it through with her earlier?

I put her through hell for over a year, and she stuck by me. No matter what.

I blinked the tears burning the back of my eyes away.

How could I ever hold anything against her?

Dahlia Ellis owned my heart. No matter what she did,

I'd always come back to her. That was how bad I had it for her.

My legs grew steadier. I blew out a breath and neared her, lifting her in my arms, the steady sound of her breathing diffusing the remnants of my anger. With Dahlia nestled against my chest, I brought her limp body to our bed, and once I'd stripped down to only my black boxer briefs, I curled my body behind her, molding myself to every inch of her. "I love you, Princess." My lips brushed the back of her shoulder before sleep claimed me.

The early sunrays blinded me through the bedroom window. Squinting, I scanned the room and saw Dahlia sound asleep in my arms, her hair bright in the morning light. My head pounded. My stomach grumbled. My mouth tasted funny. Bracing myself for one hell of a hang-over, I half-closed my eyes, cursing at myself for not closing the blinds last night when we went to bed.

My hand circled her waist and landed on her belly as I pulled her body closer. Our baby was growing in there. Cold sweat pearled on my nape. Was it even my baby? My throat closed. My lungs idled. Fuck.

As if she read my mind, Dahlia's low voice, rough from all the crying, broke the silence. "For all I know, it's yours." She placed her hand over mine, both of us cradling her tummy. "And it'll always be. I already told him that. No matter what, this baby is ours."

My body froze. My stomach turned to steel.

"But it's unfair. What if it's his? Will you ever be able to live without knowing?"

Dahlia shifted in my arms, and our gazes collided.

"I know it in my heart. Trust me. I'm not even worried." She squeezed my hand, still blanketed in hers, and offered me a peaceful and hopeful smile. "We made this little human in there. You and me. No one else."

I nodded, my emotions boiling in the depths of me, and for a moment, I feared I'd lash out at her again. I took a cleansing breath.

"Are we okay?" my girl asked in a low voice. "Or are we over?"

I cleared my throat, trying to push away the new wave of pain and anger simmering inside me.

"We'll be okay. Gimme some time to get over this. I've always feared this would happen someday. I'm hurt. So bad. And I might be for a while. But I guess it's better if you both got it out of your system. The what-if won't linger over us anymore." I ran a hand through my hair. "I can't believe I'm saying this."

Bile rose at the back of my throat.

Dahlia let out a harsh breath.

"I love you, Princess. Even if I wanted to stop loving you, I wouldn't know how. It's you and me. Forever." I took her left hand in mine and traced the edge of her engagement ring with my finger. "I still want it all. I'll forgive you. Both of you. But it might not be today. Maybe tomorrow." My lips brushed hers, and I heard the sobs bubbling from deep within her. "We'll be okay."

I unwound my body from her and stalked to the shower, needing to flush away every bit of pain clinging to me.

———

"Hey, wife, come here for a sec. I need to run something by you."

Dahlia walked in wearing nothing but one of my gray T-shirts. My Adam's apple worked at the sight. She didn't show yet, but with the pregnancy, her boobs had doubled in size. I didn't have big enough hands to contain their fullness.

My wife—we got married a week ago—propped her elbow against the doorframe, giving a peek at the side of one ass cheek. My dick came alive. I blinked. For a second, I forgot what I wanted to talk to her about.

"What's going on, husband? Have you lost your tongue, or am I the reason you're drooling right now?"

"It's not funny." I shook my head. "I don't think being infatuated over someone like I am with you is normal, Princess. You don't just mess with my body but with my head too."

Her eyes traveled down to my crotch, and she gave me an approving nod.

"I love it when you're that happy to see me. Anyway, what did you need my help with?"

I closed my eyes and inhaled, trying to put some order into my thoughts. I scanned the room, trying to remember. In the last few weeks, I'd painted the wall in a light shade of cream and the trims and door in white. Dahlia had transformed her nana's old rocking chair, stripping the pink paint and adding new white cushions, contrasting the now dark wood. A giant gray stuffed hippopotamus stood in one corner, next to the changing table and a wooden toy box. "Oh, yeah. Would you prefer the monkey mural over the crib or the changing table?"

Dahlia stepped inside the nursery with awe in her eyes. We had plenty of months left to work on the room, but somehow, I wanted it to be ready as soon as possible. It made everything more real.

"Jeff, it's beautiful." She grabbed the stuffed bear I'd laid over the pastel-yellow bedspread in the white crib. "Oh, I haven't seen this fellow in a long time. Where did you find it?"

"My mom gave me a box full of baby stuff. Jack-The-Bear was in there."

"You used to bring it every time we went camping with our parents when we were little and hid it in your sleeping bag. I knew because Carter told me."

I snickered at the memory.

"It seems like a lifetime ago that we were young and clueless. You know I was already in love with you back then. I just had no idea what the butterflies in my stomach meant."

With Jack pressed against her heart, Dahlia prowled toward me.

"The day you stared at me with heat in your eyes in your kitchen, with just a towel around your waist, changed everything for me. That's the day you stole my heart."

My hands slid under her shirt, tracing circles over her warm skin.

Dahlia shivered under the pads of my fingers.

"I'm glad I caught your eyes that day. I'd been waiting for months for you to notice me. I was desperate. I might have done that on purpose. Parade in front of you half-naked, I mean." I shrugged.

My girl's throat worked. A gleam in her eyes. Her cheeks flushed.

"I bet you did. Oh God, I didn't know what to do with all the tingles inside me. I couldn't breathe," she said with a sultry voice that made my entire body pulse with need. Her index finger trailed down from my collarbone to the waistband of my pants. "We can deal with the mural later. I kind of need you to love me right now. Those pregnancy hormones are the real deal. I keep picturing you naked—"

I scooped my wife up in my arms. "Don't say another word, Princess. I'll be your slave. Your guinea pig. Your sex toy. I'll make a sacrifice in the name of science. Let's count how many orgasms it takes to get your hormones in check."

Dahlia's smile brightened her face, and her mouth crashed on mine, mirroring all the desire pouring from every pore of my body.

15

JEFFREY

Two months later

I exited the gym, a pep in my steps. Since the day I'd learned about the baby and Dahlia agreed to marry me, I hadn't been able to stop smiling. My entire being was a twenty-four-seven-firework show. My life shone a million times brighter after we came back from Australia —except that day when I learned about Dahlia and Carter's night together. But I got over it. I had to.

Dahlia and I both had things to be ashamed of. But with love—lots of it—we worked over our differences, leaning on each other to heal our wounds.

I grabbed my phone to call my brother. I missed him.

Carter was a mess at our wedding. A drunken mess. But we both forgave him, hoping he'd come around.

Some day.

Straight to voice mail. My heart plummeted down my chest.

"Hey, Carter, it's me. Gimme a call when you get this. I love you, little bro."

I passed in front of the florist and grabbed the biggest white rose arrangement they had. Light rain tickled my skin as I made it to my car.

White Crest was rainier than usual this year. I stared at the sky, raindrops welling in my eyes, and sighed. Everything in my life finally made sense.

I pulled into the driveway, my smile still large and somehow ridiculous. I didn't care. I was happy, in love, married, and about to be a daddy.

I killed the engine, grabbed the flowers on the passenger seat, and got out of my truck.

The rain had stopped. If I looked closely, I could see the dark clouds gliding at a distance and the first stars peeking out.

My heels dug into the cobblestones in the driveway.

A layer of thick fog blanketed my vision.

I tried to breathe, but my lungs weren't working.

Cold shivers traveled from my head right down to my toes.

My hands fell at my sides, and the white rose bouquet landed on the ground in a pool of white petals.

My limbs went numb.

Darkness washed over me.

The stars in the sky didn't shine anymore.

Oxygen didn't reach my lungs—or my brain.

I tried to move but couldn't.

My heart struggled to keep beating, its rhythm now off-beat.

A big clamp pressed around my chest.

My head pounded.

Acid filled my mouth.

I tried to blink, but my eyes refused to move.

My body was failing me.

And there was nothing I could do.

Why wasn't I able to breathe on my own?

What was going on?

Burning tears streamed down my cheeks.

How did I become a prisoner of my own skin?

Heaviness grew around me, settling in all my organs.

I fought to keep my eyes open, my eyelids thick and heavy.

Images passed through my half-closed eyes.

Carter and I running around in a field, chasing butterflies.

Dahlia agreeing to be my wife.

The ultrasound where I saw our baby for the first time.

My dad teaching me how to drive.

My mom hugging me because I skinned my knee.

The first time Dahlia and I made love.

Carter shining onstage. Dahlia by his side.

The first time I saw the ocean.

My parents bringing Carter home after his birth.

The moment Dahlia said I do, tears shining in her eyes.

The day my brother and I raced in our soapbox.

Dahlia with her pigtails, twirling in her red dress.

When my eyes shut for eternity and I crumbled to the ground, all I wanted to scream was, "I'm sorry, Princess. I love you and always will. I'm so sorry. Please forgive me—"

But my dying body wouldn't let me release a single sound.

16

DAHLIA

Seconds blended into minutes. Minutes blended into hours. And hours blended into days. The world revolved around me, but I stayed there, frozen, unable to breathe.

The casket disappeared into the freshly shoveled earth, the scent of damp soil filling the air. People talked to me. Some wiped their tears.

All I could hear was my bleeding heart, fighting to stay alive.

The world revolved around me, but still, I stood there, my heels digging into the muddy ground.

The rain stopped, and rays of sunshine peeked from behind the row of magnolia trees.

With both hands, I cradled my growing belly, trying to bring some comfort to the little human growing in there.

Carter's grip around my waist fastened tight. He leaned in until his face was inches from mine. "Dah, talk to me." No words came out. My best friend pushed my hair behind my ears and cupped my face. "We need to go. Come on."

His own tears drowned most of his words. My feet

refused to move; my eyes locked on the hole in the ground before us, burying my heart forever.

Carter sobbed, and without a word, he lifted me into his arms, one arm under my knees and the other hooked under my shoulders. My head fell to his chest as sobs strangled me.

"I'll always be there for you, Dah. And the baby. You'll never be alone. We'll get through this. Together." Carter's lips lingered on my forehead. I breathed him in— cedarwood and pine—trying to let his scent soothe me as it always did. "I love you. I've always loved you, and I always will. Please lean on me. I'll have your back. I promise."

My eyes closed, and the darkness enveloped me. Carter's heartbeat played a comforting melody.

My baby deserved better than a dead father.

And I deserved better than to be a widow at twenty years old.

"I love you, Cart," I whispered as he pulled me closer to him.

In the shadow of a maple tree, we both crumpled to the rain-drenched, grassy ground, holding on to each other, our tears mixing and our hearts bleeding. Carter sat me on his lap and rested his head in the crook of my neck.

My heart disintegrated.

With two fingers, I twisted my wedding ring around.

"I'm sorry I shut you out. Both of you. It's all my fault—"

I pulled Carter's head to my chest and raked my fingers through his hair. "Cart, we both did stuff we're not proud of. But this wasn't your fault. It wasn't. Don't blame yourself. Sudden cardiac arrests happen. All the time."

Clinging to each other, we cried until we had no more tears left.

And then we cried some more because we both had lost a huge slice of our hearts.

Forever.

EPILOGUE

DAHLIA

Three years later

I caught sight of myself in the mirror facing the dressing rooms. In the last three years, I felt like I'd aged thirty years. At twenty-three, I'd lived many lives already. The one before fame, the one when I was part of Carter Hills Band, and the after-Carter-Hills-Band —where I became a widow and a single mother in the stretch of a few months. When I quit the band, after that show in Australia three years ago, I never thought it'd be the smartest decision of my life. The one that would carve the rest of my life's path. Never would I have thought life was giving me an out to spend the much-needed time with my fiancé turned husband before he dropped dead at the same age as I was now.

I slid the back of my hand across my forehead, wiping off pearls of sweat. The store was looking good, but I had still many hours left to put in before the big opening.

"All done," Carter said as he picked Jack up in his arms. My little man wound his arms around his uncle's neck. "You and I, we're going home, buddy. Give Mama some time alone. I think she deserves it." He turned to face me. "All the boxes are here. You won't have to do any heavy lifting."

After Jeff passed, Carter cleaned up his act and stepped in as a father figure for Jack. After all these years, we were still best friends.

I named my son after his daddy's stuffed bear—Jack-the-Bear. The one that brought Jeff joy, comfort, and peace while growing up.

"How will I ever be able to thank you?"

Carter winked. "You could kiss me. For old time's sake," he said, half-serious, half-joking.

I slapped his arm. "Don't be silly, we were never meant to be together."

Carter's smirk vanished from his handsome face. His eyes were still the color of the sea before a storm, but now his face was more angular, his cheekbones higher, and his mass of dark hair gave the man he became a boyish look. When I looked at my son, I saw both Carter and Jeff in him. He was the perfect mix of them both. My heart flipped every time I thought about it.

I still believed Jeff was Jack's biological father, but there was still a possibility he wasn't. I gave Carter the result of the paternity test in a sealed envelope after my son's birth, but he hadn't opened it yet. Or I didn't think he had.

I sighed and draped my arms around the two most important men in my life.

"You know I'm right. One day you'll realize I'm not the one for you. But I'll always be your best friend. No matter what. You're stuck with me, Cart. And I'm stuck with you. We're family. Forever. Nothing else matters."

Carter closed his eyes for a minute, pressing his forehead to mine, and sucked in a breath. "Maybe one day you'll be the one realizing we were actually meant to be together." Something passed through his melted-steel gray irises. "We don't need to talk about it right now. This little man needs to be fed and put to bed for a nap."

Carter's lips brushed my cheek.

"You two behave, okay?"

"Okay, Mama," my baby boy said with the cutest smile, his chubby cheeks glistening in the light of my shop. My shop. I still had a hard time believing it was real.

"Come home when you're done, Dah. I'll cook dinner. You need a night off. We'll be at my place."

I nodded, too tired to argue. Carter was right. I needed to take care of myself for a change.

"I'll see you both later."

I kissed Jack on the head and walked my family outside. It wasn't even noon, and the sun was already shining high on Green Mountain. I loved spring. Flowers. Grass. Sunshine grazing skin. It filled me with so much happiness.

My gaze traveled around Main Street. People were roaming around, enjoying their day, gathering in front of all those cafés, ready for lunch.

In our little town, Main Street was the place to be. During the summer months, it filled with tourists. All year round, it was the busiest place in Green Mountain. Looking for a restaurant? Main Street. Grocery shopping? Main Street. General store? Main Street. And soon, looking for a wedding or evening gown? Dahlia's Bridal Shop. On Main Street.

I relaxed my shoulders and breathed in the warm air. Every spring felt like a new chapter in my life. As if everything could be possible once the warm weather chased the winter away.

Full of hope—and joy—I turned on my heels and

walked back inside my store. It looked charming. The walls had been painted a shade of powder blue, and the ceilings were made of recycled dark wooden planks. The dressing rooms, circling a white pedestal with a three-panel floor-to-ceiling mirror, bore silvery curtains. It was everything I'd ever dreamed it would be. A princess's kingdom, as Mama would say. This morning, I received boxes of gowns and wanted to hang most of them by the end of the day.

It was a miracle Carter came back to town, before going to Europe next week, at the same moment I desperately needed his help with Jack. He always appeared on my doorstep when I needed him the most. I liked to think that Jeff was guiding Carter, helping me from wherever he was.

My parents still lived in White Crest, so I saw them every few months. And usually, I was the one driving there, instead of them coming here, which, with a two-year-old, complicated things a little. But hey, I was the one who moved to Green Mountain when my life burned to ashes after Jeff's death and the press found out about the pregnancy and assumed the nastiest of things.

I couldn't stay in our home.

The ghosts from our past were impossible to chase.

I needed a fresh start. A place to call my own.

Carter bought a mountaintop piece of land last year and built a cabin up there. He lived in Nashville most of the time but always came back here to unwind and spend time with Jack and me whenever he could.

The bell over the door chimed.

"Hey, Cart. Did you forget something?" I hung the dress in my hands and turned around. I halted. The man standing in front of me looked nothing like Carter Hills.

Blond hair, broad shoulders, tanned skin.

My heart jumped in my chest. Warmth enveloped all

my senses. I tried to speak, but I stood there like a fool instead, eyeing the man in front of me.

"Hey," he said, his eyes taking me in. A spark gleamed in his golden irises, the color of honey.

I wet my lips with my tongue and swallowed. "Hey."

We stared at each other for a few beats, neither of us brave enough to break the silence or eye contact. I linked my hands together and fidgeted with my fingers.

I was cast under a spell, and I had no clue what I should do. I knew nothing except I liked the feeling. My heart hummed. The rock that had been pressing over my chest for the last three years fractured.

I studied the man. Square chin, symmetrical face, a scar crossing his left eyebrow.

He cleared his throat. "I'm sorry to bother you. I just moved here, and I'm not really familiar with the town yet." He looked around, then cast a glance at the paper in his hand. "So, I guess you're not Hilton and Sons, the construction business?" He tipped one dark-blond brow, and a dimple appeared on his chin as he smiled at me. The paper in his hand shook, and the man folded it in four and stuffed it—along with his hand—in the pocket of his dark pants. His other hand raked through his hair, messing up the locks.

I studied him.

Was this stranger always nervous, or did I make him nervous?

I swallowed hard and pushed my copper braid behind my shoulder.

My heart did a somersault in my chest. Like it had just woken up after a three-year-long harsh winter.

"Hilton is on Elk Road, not Main Street." I clamped my hands together to avoid fidgeting.

The man scratched the side of his head. "And where is Elk Road? I'm a bit lost."

"Give me a minute. I'll lock the shop and walk you there. It's not that far."

"Are you sure? I don't want to be a bother—"

I shrugged. "I insist. Fresh air will do me good. And it's a shame to be stuck inside when the weather is that great outside. I've been in the store fifteen hours a day for the last month. I'm in dire need of some vitamin C." I let out a weird giggle.

"I think you mean vitamin D—"

My face heated up.

"Yeah. Vitamin D. You're right."

We found our pace as we strolled down the street.

"I'm Nick, by the way." My body purred at the sound of his voice, all gravelly and soft. It woke up something in me. I could listen to him talk for hours.

"I'm Dahlia." I pinched my lips together and tucked a loose strand of hair behind my ear, trying to avoid saying something stupid. "We're here," I said when we stopped in front of the two-storied, red-bricked building.

Nick pivoted on his heels to face me.

"I just have to sign a few documents. I'm starting here as a carpenter next week. It'll only take a couple of minutes. Would you care to wait for me? We could grab a coffee or something. I'm starving, and the sights and smells of all those restaurants on Main Street did nothing to tame my hunger." Nick offered me a hopeful smile. "Unless you're too busy at the store and having lunch with me will make you late."

My fingers found the wedding ring I wore in a chain around my neck and twirled it around.

I inhaled, trying to look calm and in control.

"I'd like that."

"Great." Nick squeezed my upper arm. My blood warmed up at his touch. Tingles ran along my spine. "Wait for me. I won't be long."

Our eyes met for a beat, and for the first time in three years, I let out the breath I'd been holding in. His large hand brushed my shoulder for a split second as he rounded me to enter the building, and a jolt of electricity shot through me.

———

"Dah, you don't even know this guy. You're sure it's a good idea to go on a date with him? You met him like what? Once? Are you sure he's not after your money? Or maybe he's a serial killer?"

I sighed and pushed Carter back with both hands as he joined me in the kitchen.

"C'mon, Cart. I haven't dated since Jeff—I'm still young. I'm allowed to go out. And the last time I checked, you weren't my daddy."

I hated it when Carter became too protective of me. Which he did daily since his brother passed. Even when he was on the other side of the world, we talked almost every day. Carter checked on me first. Then on Jack. And then on me again.

My best friend erased the distance between us and cupped my face with his hands. "I'm sorry, Dah. I don't like you going out with a stranger. You refuse to date me, but you agree to go out with someone you've just met."

"Oh God, Carter. You're impossible. Not again. You and I, not happening. We're so much better as friends. And I would never risk our friendship for anything. And I spent hours with Nick the other day. We clicked. I can't explain it, but I felt it. He's harmless. Don't worry about me. I'm a big girl. I've been through hell and made my way back. I'm sure I can survive a date with a guy who's charming, smart, and interesting."

Carter raised his hands in surrender. "Okay. Fine. Do as you wish. But promise to call me if you need a ride. Or if the date is a disaster."

I bobbed my head, sliding one hand along his chest. "Thanks. And I appreciate you watching Jack tonight."

We exchanged one of our wordless smiles, and I kissed his cheek. Carter wrapped his arms around me, and we stayed there, both of us comforting each other's soul.

I peeled myself from his embrace at the sound of the doorbell. For a second, I thought my heart would melt on the floor.

When was the last time I felt so giddy? Too long ago to remember.

I stopped breathing as I opened the door under Carter's watchful eyes.

"Hey, you look beautiful," Nick said as a greeting, before leaning in and placing a chaste kiss on my cheek, then stepping in.

I took in Nick's dark denims, brown shoes, and long-sleeved black shirt, hugging his firm chest and broad shoulders. His hair was gelled away from his forehead. He didn't just look handsome, he smelled good too. Woodsy and fresh.

"You don't look so bad yourself." I failed at containing the grin taking over my face.

Jack ran in my direction and tangled his little body around my leg. "Mama." I ruffled his dark hair before squatting to level my gaze with his.

"You be a nice boy tonight, baby. I love you. Keep an eye on Carter for me," I said with a wink. Jack giggled. The best sound in the entire world. "You know Carter needs your help to stay out of trouble." I lifted him into my arms and hugged him for a long minute, breathing his baby-scent in, as I nuzzled his neck.

Carter stood there, silent, both thumbs hooked into his pockets. After giving me one of his "be careful" stares, he lifted Jack into his arms. With heavy steps, he neared Nick —hovering over him by a few inches—and held out his hand. Using his most severe tone, he said, "Hi. I'm Carter. Nice to meet you."

"Nice to meet you too. Heard a lot about you," my date said, shaking his hand.

"Please treat Dahlia with the respect she deserves."

"I wouldn't do anything less. I'll be a perfect gentleman," Nick said, his eyes locked on Carter, not shaken up by the threat.

I backhanded my best friend on the shoulder. "Really, Cart?"

Carter offered me his panties-melting grin, as the press had named his most-adorable-slash-innocent smile —the one he used on me whenever we disagreed about something and he tried to win me over—and a shrug. His stupid grin had no effect on me. None. I brushed it away and looked at him with batting eyelashes instead, my own version of puppy eyes. The one I knew he couldn't resist.

"Okay. Fine. You two have fun. Better?"

Game over. I won.

Nick snickered behind his hand.

"Yep. Much better." I kissed Jack's head and followed Nick to his car, his hand on the small of my back the entire time, under Carter's heavy stare. "I'm sorry about Carter. He's a little overprotective."

Nick stopped and turned to face me. "It's okay, Dahlia. I would be overprotective of you if I were in his shoes. I think it's great that you can count on him." I stood there, speechless.

My heart danced in my chest.

Something intangible burned between us. It filled the air.

I had no idea what it was, but for once, in a very long time, I had hope that my future wouldn't be so gray and dull anymore. That a rainbow could appear after the storm.

Nick opened the door of his dark-blue truck for me and helped me in.

Our gazes fused together. A smile stretched across his face. My pulse raced.

"Ready?" he asked as he settled behind the wheel.

"Totally," I said, mirroring his smile. The clouds parted, and the sun shone on me again.

To be continued in *Cruel Destiny*...

emmanuellesnow.com/cruel-destiny

Thank you for reading Jeff and Dahlia's heartbreaking and beautiful love story.

If you like this book, please talk about it and post a review. This is the best way to help me find new readers who would love it too and keep written amazing and touching love stories.

————

The **Second Tear** duet follows Nick's story before he met Dahlia followed by their love story. It's one of those stories that will live in your heart forever. Keep reading for an excerpt and bonus content.

Read ***Cruel Destiny*** now

or read the full-length duet, ***Second Tear***, here

emmanuellesnow.com/second-tear

———

FREE bonus chapter
Want even more? Your bonus chapter awaits here
emmanuellesnow.com/bonus-content

THANK YOU
DID YOU ENJOY THIS BOOK?

Thank you so much for reading Dahlia and Jeff's story. If you enjoyed reading this book, please help spread the word about it. **Each review**—as brief as it might be—is **invaluable** in **helping me** pursue my career as a full-time writer.

Please, for other readers' sake, avoid spoilers in your reviews.

I'm really lucky to count you as a reader, and I truly appreciate your support.

Emmanuelle

ACKNOWLEDGMENTS

I wrote Dahlia's story in three days. I didn't plan on writing it, but once I started, the words wouldn't stop pouring out of me. There was so much love in this book that I got super emotional every time I read it. Jeff and Dahlia were so perfect together (sorry, Carter), even if their journey wasn't smooth sailing all the time. They loved each other with all they had, and their love was so powerful, it helped them to overcome every challenge they faced along the way.

That's what true love is all about! Isn't it?

But don't be sad as you reach the end. Nick is a great guy, and he and Dahlia are good together.

She can still get her happy ending. It will just be different than the one she starts her journey with.

You'll get to hear the rest of their story in Nick's book, which is coming out soon.

I want to thank my husband, without whom I wouldn't have embarked on this journey. Your support, your love, and your confidence in me never cease to amaze me. And make me smile. I love you with every piece of my heart.

I also want to thank my kids. All four of them. Every time I come up with a new story, you always want to know more. You might not be old enough to read my books yet, but you're the best spokespersons an author (and a mom) can get. The way you discuss my characters, as if they are real, and express your opinion about them is magical. Please never stop. Thanks, guys, for being my biggest fans. But sorry, you're not allowed to take my books to school…

I also want to thank two people who are important to me. Virginie: Every time I talk to you, I end up smiling. Merci beaucoup pour tout. Shalini: What would I do without you? Thanks for crying with me (yeah, this book is a tearjerker!) and for your precious talent with words that make my stories shine. I'm always excited when I get the story back from you.

To my readers, thank you for your support and love. None of this would be possible without you. You are giving me the chance to write my stories, and for that, I'll be eternally grateful.

And to the bloggers who have shared *Sweet Agony* with the rest of the world, a million times over: thank you.

To all of you, cheers!

ABOUT THE AUTHOR

Smart, Sexy, and Sassy Love Stories

USA Today and International Bestselling author Emmanuelle Snow is a contemporary author of mature YA and New Adult love stories, who gives life to strong characters who'll fight with all they have to reach their life goals and find their own happiness.

Emmanuelle is in love with love. Especially complicated, deep, and passionate feelings that make a relationship extraordinary and complex all at the same time.

In her spare time, when she's not writing or reading, she likes to go on road trips—with her four kids and her own soulmate—watch movies, paint, or do some DIY, always with a cup of green tea in her hand and listening to country music.

She splits her time between beautiful Canada and the small US towns she adores.

Find all of Emmanuelle's books here:
emmanuellesnow.com/books

———

Want to connect with Emmanuelle online?

ALSO BY THE AUTHOR

CARTER HILLS BAND UNIVERSE

(suggested reading order)

Carter Hills Band series

False Promises

HEART SONG DUET

BlindSided

ForeverMore

Whiskey Melody series

Sweet Agony

SECOND TEAR DUET

Cruel Destiny

Beautiful Salvation

BREATHLESS DUET

Wild Encounter

Brittle Scars

Upon A Star series

Last Hope

Midnight Sparks

Love Song For Two series

LONESOME STAR DUET

Fallen Legend

Rising Star

Read them all

emmanuellesnow.com/books

Available on author's bookshop

emmanuellesnowshop.com

CRUEL DESTINY

NICK

My knuckles rapped on the ajar door, pushing it open when the words "Come on in" resonated from inside the room. Murielle, Derek's mom, gestured for me to join them.

"Nick," the boy exclaimed, a permanent smile etched on his face, as if his life was fucking fantastic.

"How are you doing, big guy?" I asked, quirking an eyebrow at him, pulling my lips into a warm smile when we fist-bumped.

"Amazing. Look at this," my little friend said, pulling a red jersey from the side, pride gushing out from every pore of his being. "Barry Hamilton came over this morning."

"The hockey player?" I asked.

"Yeah. He's so huge. Cory Black and Rory Dupont came too."

I smoothed the polyester fabric of the shirt between my fingers, taking in all the signatures written in black ink.

"Man, this is awesome. The entire team signed this?"

Derek bobbed his head, stars twinkling in his eyes, his

grin stretching to both ears. "And we took pictures too. Show Nick, Mom. Show him."

Murielle handed me her phone, and I swept through the dozens of pictures with the pad of my thumb. My heart frizzled in my chest. I blinked, pushing my emotions down. Derek didn't deserve me being an emotional mess beside him. He needed my strength. And my unconditional optimism.

"Man, this is pretty cool." I lifted the paper bag I'd dropped on the edge of the bed when I walked in. "Thought you and I could have lunch together, you know, just us guys. I've had a shitty week—oops, sorry," I said, wrinkling my face and offering Murielle an apologetic smile.

Derek let out a heartfelt laugh. "I'm not six anymore, Nick. It's okay, I won't repeat it."

His mother rose to her feet. "Since Nick is here, I'll take an hour or two to run some errands. You boys be good, okay?" She turned to face her twelve-year-old. "You all right, baby?"

Derek nodded, the smile still anchored to his face as if every day was the most amazing one in his short life.

"Make sure you keep Nick out of trouble."

The boy's laughter reverberated through the small room. And it multiplied when I shrugged. Murielle gave a headshake and spun to face me. "Can you stay until I'm back?"

"Sure. My entire Sunday afternoon is dedicated to my friend here. I'm not going anywhere."

She squeezed my upper arm and bowed her head before walking out of the room, her lips pressed together in a thin line. I knew the look. Something was going on. It was in the air. Thick and barbed. With a grin plastered across my face, I tried my best to avoid bringing the subject up while Derek could hear us. It could wait. *Later*, I reiterated to myself.

With a soft thud, I landed my ass on the chair Murielle vacated seconds ago and fished the food from the bag. Greasy cheeseburgers, seasoned fries, extra-large sodas—root beer with no ice for my young friend, just the way he liked it. I knew Derek wasn't supposed to eat junk food. But I'd asked his doctors a few months ago, and they agreed he could use some fun in his life. And if it meant eating burgers or tacos with me once a week, then so be it. Even Murielle concurred.

Derek lifted his cup and clinked it to mine. "Thanks for the burger, bro."

I coughed, almost choking on the pieces of fries in my mouth. "Bro?" I repeated, taking a sip to alleviate the itchy feeling in my throat.

Derek shrugged and ended up giggling. Like a kid should always do. "Saw it in a movie last night. Sounded nice. Since we're best friends, I thought it fitting."

I swallowed hard. Sometimes I forgot I was the closest thing Derek had to a friend. His peers from school had stopped visiting a year ago. Kids his age ought to be running around on a soccer field or riding bikes, chasing frogs or going to camp, not stuck in a hospital bed, bald, skinny, alone all year round. It wasn't fair. None of this was how childhood should be.

My eyes found a picture of us by his bed, back when I coached his Little League team, before cancer, smiling on the field with matching golden jerseys and unruly blond hair. A mixture of emotions swirled inside me. I remembered that day as if it were yesterday. When we used to be carefree.

I swiveled my gaze to my friend and mirrored his smile.

"I'm fine with bro if that's what you want. What do I call you from now on then?"

Derek sighed. Like the pre-teen he was. "Bro. C'mon. If I call you bro, you call me bro. That's how it works, no?"

I nodded. "I guess." Bro wasn't a word I used with Tucker and Jace. We usually called each other *man*. "Bro's fine, bro."

After a game of chess, which Derek won, as always—this kid was smart beyond words—he asked in a small voice, needing the reassurance of my presence, "If I take a nap, will you be there when I wake up?"

I nodded.

There was no other place I'd rather be. Since we'd known each other, this kid had touched my heart in countless ways. I didn't have it in me to refuse him anything. Minutes later, the sound of his steady breathing filled the air, and my heartbeat kicked up. A nagging feeling clawed my spine, crushing each vertebra. Derek could bring much-required sunshine to this world in the way he beamed and left a permanent mark on those he blessed with his presence rather than being stuck in this room, glued to a bed, too weak to get up. A dark cloud hovered over me each time the thoughts ran freely through my head. With a deep inhale, I scanned the room, pushing all my gloomy reflections as far as I could. Over the last year, Murielle had decorated the walls with her paintings and framed family pictures. The hospital allowed it. Since cancer hit Derek five years ago, this room had become a second home to him. Between surgeries, radiation, chemo, and an endless list of infections, he now lived here full time.

My gaze lingered on his taut face as he slept. Pain dodged his footsteps and won most days. Purple rings shadowed his eyes. In the last year, they had lost their vibrant blue color and were now more a dull shade of gray after everything his body went through. A baseball cap covered his bald head. My eyes drifted to a picture on the wall. A six-year-old Derek blowing candles on his birthday cake, the same smile he bore earlier today, lighting up his healthy little boy's face. A weight grew in my chest, pressing against my lungs, suffocating me. Nowadays Derek's skin looked pasty white—almost translucent—having lost its rosy tone.

The boy was dying. I could feel it. My soul recognized the signs as my body ached at the realization. Chills ran through me, involuntary tremors shaking me. The sight of him brought back the memories of watching my father fight cancer when I was fifteen. But my father survived. Derek wouldn't.

I put the remnants of our lunch back in the paper bag and took everything to the trash can next to the bed.

My gaze lingered on the boy I'd got attached to over the years. Each time I had time off, I swung by the hospital to spend a few hours with him. It felt important. Filling my lungs with quivering inhales, I pinched the bridge of my nose, fighting the emotional storm spiraling inside me that threatened to shatter the facade I usually wore in his presence.

Memories of my time spent with him resurfaced. A tiny smile tugged at my lips.

I was barely seventeen when I met him on the field before one of our Little League games for the first time. From that day on, I'd stuck by his side. His spirit of the game, his cheerfulness, the glow in him drew me in. He was always eager to learn more, always giving his best. We connected big time during those games. Soon Derek felt like a little brother to me. Murielle, being a single mom, often ran late to pick him up after practice. He and I started hanging out together while we waited for her, eating ice cream from the truck parked next to the baseball field, chatting about school and his friends. In more ways than one, from that moment, Murielle and Derek became my second family.

I watched him the nights Murielle had to work double shifts at the restaurant.

Sometimes I'd invite him to throw the ball with Tucker, Jace, and me.

Once a week, Murielle would have me over for dinner after my parents left town so I wouldn't feel left out. Because four months after I turned eighteen, my folks moved to Italy. A dream they both cherished. One they had been caressing for years. But also, one I didn't share. They asked me to come with them. My younger sister, Jessica, did. I refused. My life was in Chicago. My friends were here. And as much as living in Europe sounded awesome, just the idea of going away would knot my stomach in a tight bundle back then.

This was my home. I loved it here. Instead of chasing other people's dreams, I chose to cherish mine. Because I only had one shot at this life, I wanted to make mine count. On my own terms. I got a job, worked my ass off to get experience, showed my commitment and integrity, and secured my own money. So far, my plan had worked great.

Two years after we met, Derek began chemotherapy. All his hair—including his eyebrows—fell off, and he kept fighting. Thinner and frailer through the battle, he never lost that mischievous spark shining in him.

Still on that bed, his breathing shallow and his frame delicate, I could picture the healthy boy he had been. Because no matter how the illness changed his appearance, it never altered his essence. It shone bright like the scintillating gem he was.

A long huff escaped my tight lips. My eyes stayed anchored to Derek's figure.

Murielle came back at the exact moment. She touched my side, her tiny hand feather-light against my muscles. "Thank you for spending time with him," she whispered, her loving eyes resting on her son's recumbent form, so small under the covers I'd adjusted for him.

I shoved my hands in my pockets, my shoulders sagging forward. "What's the prognosis?" A lump grew in my throat, and I pushed it down to even up my breathing. I could do this. I had to know. I deserved to know. No matter how bad the truth would hurt.

Murielle cast a glance down and took a wheezing breath before meeting my eyes. "Not good. A few weeks at the most. If at all. His body can't take it anymore. His white blood cell count is too low. He's tired. The last infection drained all the energy reserves in him. He doesn't want to fight anymore. We talked about it. He says he's ready to go."

I wiped the tears building in my eyes with my thumb.

"It's unfair. I'm so sorry." I shifted around to wrap a defeated Murielle in my arms, rocking her back and forth. I'd do anything to stop the heartbreaking, silent sobs coming out of her. Her shoulders heaved in my embrace. Nothing I could say would make this moment less painful, so I kept my mouth shut, my throat constricting painfully with unshed tears.

————

Hours later, after I promised Derek to visit the next day, I slouched my ass on a bar stool, my fingers knitted together on my nape, my elbows anchored to the worn ebony counter as I tried to wrap my brain around all the jumbled-up emotions in my head. And my heart.

Tucker, my best friend since we were five, lightly punched my arm and slid onto the stool next to mine.

"I knew I'd find you here. Bad day?"

I huffed before turning my head to stare at him. "Derek. He's dying. For real this time. Nothing the doctors can do. It's over. He's done fighting."

"How long?" he asked, motioning the bartender over with a flick of his hand. "We'll have two more of those," he said to the man, pointing to the empty tumbler before me.

"Weeks. A month or two at the most."

"Sorry, man. I know how much you love that kid. Life is fucking unfair. In which world do children have to fight for their lives? It's a freaking joke." Tucker shook his head and guzzled half the drink the bartender brought over.

"He asked me if I would look after his mom." Moisture welled behind my eyeballs, stinging the already raw emotions lingering there.

Tuck glided his finger into his shirt collar and cracked his neck before loosening the navy tie.

"Fuck," was all he said. Yeah, no other powerful word could translate the feeling we all shared.

In silence, we sipped our drinks while my best friend gestured to the bartender for another round.

"Make them double this time."

The bartender nodded and turned to grab the whiskey bottle we'd surely empty tonight.

After another minute of silence, where we each ruminated over the unsaid words floating between us, Tuck cleared his throat as his somber eyes fixated on mine. "How's Murielle?"

The lining of my throat hurt as if a million needles

prickled the flesh. And it wasn't from the liquor we'd been drinking. I blinked fast, pleading my emotions to settle and prevent the tears from blinding me. If Derek could be strong facing a death sentence, then I had to be too. Only then could I support his mother when she'd need me the most. My gaze drifted to a table where a group of women was celebrating one of their milestone birthdays. Big silver balloons, a two and a five, were attached to the back of a chair, and a dozen cherry-red shot glasses spread on the table. The birthday girl rocked a white top and a teal crown, her smile huge and expectant for the years to come. As if nothing could shadow this moment. I used to be that guy. Years ago. Before I understood life was a flimsy line that could fray any moment and shatter everything in its wake. A shake of my head and I swigged down half my drink in one go and focused my attention back on my friend.

"A wreck. The worst part is I couldn't say anything to lessen the pain. For once, I couldn't find the words." I sank my face into my hands and dropped my shoulders with a loud sigh. "What are you supposed to tell a mother who's about to lose her only child?"

"Nothing, I guess."

I brought my whiskey to my lips, enjoying the trail of fire down my throat, reminding me I was still alive.

And about to get wasted.

———

Read Nick and Dahlia's story,
Cruel Destiny, now

https://emmanuellesnow.com/cruel-destiny

Author's bookstore at emmanuellesnowshop.com

"This is a novel with so much depth, so much heart and so much love. There is steam, there is loss and there are moments of shock." (Book.ish Julie)

"Emmanuelle has done it yet again. She found a way to slip into my mind and heart with her words and the creation of characters you can't help but fall in love with." (The Cozy Pages blog)

"A book that made me smile through my tears... Read the book with your heart as only Ms. Snow can break it as well as glue it back together. Emotions are her forte. And she get me every single time." (Book reviews by Shalini)

Cruel Destiny is book one in the
Second Tear duet.

https://emmanuellesnow.com/cruel-destiny

WILD ENCOUNTER
ADDISON

I slumped down on the couch of the posh hotel we were staying all weekend and huffed, a wine bottle hanging from my fingers by its neck. Glasses were overrated, anyway. "That's it. I'm over men. I'm done." My childhood best friend snickered. "I'm serious, Dah. This time I mean it. You know I do."

I scanned the space around me. Large windows with a direct view of Nashville's busy streets below, high wooden beam ceilings, dark flooring, and handcrafted wood furniture. Chic and tasteful, with an unmistakable country vibe.

"Yeah, right. I'm sure you won't last a week. Two at the most," Dahlia teased.

My friend, and the bride-to-be, inched closer, and I zipped her up. Her cut-out mermaid gown was a gray-lavender hue and looked both sexy and demure, showing just enough skin without being indecent. Perfectly Dahlia Ellis.

Before I could return to my lazy position on the couch, she beckoned me with a finger to follow her. Sitting on the edge of the bathtub, I glugged the wine straight from the bottle and watched her apply mascara.

"Addi, there are good men out there who would appreciate your light. Don't punish all of them because you dated a few who were total dickheads." She grinned at her reflection. But it was meant for me. And it warmed my heart as she continued, "I'm confident you won't last in your quest to ignore them all when they turn on the charm."

"Laugh all you want, girlfriend. You'll see. Be prepared to be shocked. This time, I'm not backing down. Anyway, remember Felicia from college? She messaged me last week. It's destiny."

"The one you 'experimented' with?" my friend asked, curving her fingers into elaborate air quotes, her gaze fixed on her eyelashes in the mirror, not sparing me a look.

Another sip. "The same. We could have been in love and lived happily ever after. The timing was just not right."

"Huh, you said the same thing about Carter once. Besides, I thought women weren't your thing," Dahlia added with a quirked brow.

"It's not the same. And perhaps I changed my mind. Who knows? I might be into women more than men after all. Think about it, we should have been a couple, you and I. Everything would have been much simpler."

"You think?"

I shrugged. "We get along fine. And we're friends, so our relationship would have had a solid foundation. Look at you and Nick. Friends, then lovers. I believe that's the secret to long-lasting love. Back to business..." I sighed. "Felicia and I experienced some pretty memorable moments together. It's just Shawn happened to cross my path, and I couldn't resist him. Stupid me. Stupid men. I'm telling you their species is old news. You're lucky you found two awesome ones in your lifetime. What are the odds? God knows I've tried. I usually don't back down easily, but hey, maybe it's time I try something else. That I understand once and for all what life has been trying to tell me all these years—"

Dahlia shook her head, focusing her attention on me for the first time since I started the conversation about my disastrous love life. "Addi, you know how much I love it when you're not being overdramatic."

I poked my tongue out, and we both burst out laughing. Peace washed over me. Dahlia Ellis had that effect on me. Her presence was enough to ease my doubts. And bring a curve to my lips even when I didn't feel like expressing joy. "That's why you love me. I'm entertaining. Despite myself. Anyway, where are the bridal shower festivities taking place? I can't wait to party the entire weekend. The distraction will do me good."

Dahlia reached over and landed a kiss on my cheek, her eyes searching mine. Worry shimmered in them. "You okay?"

I nodded.

"You'd tell me if it wasn't the case, right?" I sensed the apprehension in her question.

"Always. You're the only one I willingly confide in."

With a warm smile that promised everything would turn out just fine, she went back to applying her makeup. "All over town. Tonight, we're having dinner with only the people closest to us. And tomorrow, a get-together with some of my good friends and the guys on a yacht before splitting up and maybe meeting them again later."

"Rewind for a sec. We're having your bridal shower with your future husband and his friends?"

"Yep. His best friend. Guys from work. That's the idea."

"Yeah, I should've been the one organizing the whole thing." Dahlia raised a hand, ready to argue, but I kept going. "For what it's worth, I'm sorry I let you down. I was really looking forward to throwing you the bachelorette party of the century."

A new weight grew heavy on my shoulders. In the fog of my latest relationship blowing up, I had lost focus on what really mattered. This time, my tears had knocked me out more than ever. But I was back now. And no way was I failing the girl I considered a sister again.

Dahlia pulled me into a hug. "It's okay. Don't chastise yourself. It'll still be fun. And you did plan most of the wedding already. You deserve a night off. To enjoy yourself. You, me, booze, music. And the man I love and his friends."

I leaned back, studying her for a moment. Dahlia had no ounce of evilness in her. She really meant everything she'd just said.

"What is it?" she asked, a frown marring her forehead.

"Real sweet, Dah. After I told you I was done with men, you're going to make me spend hours with a bunch of Nick's buddies. And alcohol. If I didn't know your heart, I'd think this was a test. To check my newfound determination." One more sip of the wine. *Be strong, Addi,* I repeated in my head. I flicked my hand and pasted a smile on my lips. "Know what? Doesn't matter. I won't back down. I'm done with men, and I'll prove it to you. Tonight. I won't flirt, and I won't kiss. Nope. Nada. D.O.N.E. Just watch and learn, girlfriend."

I held out my hand, and we shook on it.

Read Tucker and Addison's story,
Wild Encounter, now

emmanuellesnow.com/wild-encounter

Author's bookstore at emmanuellesnowshop.com

"Tucker freaking Philips!!! Wow! Emmanuelle Snow has written another beautiful, rollercoaster, sneakily emotional romance."
(Goodreads)

"This is without a doubt Emmanuelle's best work yet!" (Goodreads)

Wild Encounter is book one in the ***Breathless*** duet.
emmanuellesnow.com/wild-encounter

Made in United States
North Haven, CT
20 May 2023